Stories 2000

WALES AND THE WORLD

A collection of stories over
the centuries

from the Bible to Bala,
from Canaan to Wales.

Collected by
Aled Davies

CYHOEDDIADAU'R
GAIR

℗ Cyhoeddiadau'r Gair 1999

Collected by Aled Davies.
Contributions from: H. Gareth Alban, Huw John Hughes, Cynthia
Davies, Margaret Cynfi, Brenda Wyn Jones, Elfed ap Nefydd
Roberts, Caryl Parry Jones, Mici Plwm, Angharad Tomos, T. Llew
Jones, Martyn Geraint, Dafydd Iwan, Wynford Ellis Owen, Roy
Noble, Arfon Haines Davies, Maldwyn Thomas, Elenid Jones, the
children of Manod Primary school, Blaenau Ffestiniog.

The publishers acknowledge the support and co-operation of
Scripture Union and *Angus Hudson Ltd.*
Printed in the U.K.

ISBN 1 85994 216 4

Published by:
Cyhoeddiadau'r Gair, Cyngor Ysgolion Sul Cymru,
Ysgol Addysg, PCB, Safle'r Normal,
Bangor, Gwynedd, LL57 2PX.

Contents

(m) What's the Millennium?

2000 years since what...?

The Dome!

The biggest party ever!

Millennium bugs!

Why all the fuss about the beginning of the year 2000? Is it all an excuse for television presenters and the tourist industry to go mad? Won't your life be exactly the same on 1 January 2000 as it was on 31 December 1999?

Yes, it will, unless the rumours are right about the bug, traffic lights being out of time, cars not starting, aeroplanes being grounded, etc. But apart from that...

It's easy to forget the real reason why there is anything to celebrate at all. So this book begins with the past, with lots of information about Jesus, whose birth two thousand years ago (or thereabouts) is the real reason for the party. In the present, there are extracts of stories people read today, which have been influenced by the life of Jesus. And then we've asked lots of people to look to the future, to tell us what present they would give to a child born on 1 January 2000.

We hope you enjoy reading Stories for the Millennium. Keep it as your Millennium souvenir!

Have a great future!

(m) So what is the Millennium?

The Millennium is a great opportunity to mark the passing of time. But that's not the whole point of it....

What do people still remember about Jesus from 2000 years ago?

- A man who has had more impact on history than any other individual.
- The things he did, which have been learned and copied for 2000 years.
- The things he said, which have been studied and understood for 2000 years.
- The amazing story of Jesus coming alive after being put to death on a cross.
- The fact that Jesus said he will always be with all people for all time.

What happened in 1 AD?

- Jesus may have been born. (More likely, he was born four or five years earlier.)
- Other people were born, others died.
- Wars were fought and peace was found. (Julius Caesar had come and gone in the British Isles. He didn't like the weather!)
- The Celts had also invaded the British Isles...and they stayed.
- The Romans ruled Israel. They held a population count. Everyone who lived in the Roman Empire had to take part. That included Israel.

So people remember Jesus. The Millennium is about his 2000th birthday. Read on to find out how it all started...

Dear Friends,

It's been such a hard and strange year for us. First of all we (that's my wife Mary, and I) were both visited by an angel. That shook us up, I can tell you. The angel told us we'd have a child who would be a boy. We were even given his name - Jesus! Then, even though Mary was pregnant and pretty large, we travelled to Bethlehem for the census. That's because the Romans were collecting everyone's name. We couldn't find anywhere to sleep. We ended up staying in a cold, dirty and smelly animal shed.

Late one night, our son was born. We were startled when a crowd of shepherds just turned up. They'd heard about our son, Jesus, so left their sheep and came to worship him. Then a bit later, along came some wise men. They had travelled a great distance and brought very expensive gifts.

Jesus was a few months old when we had to escape to Egypt (a long, long, way away). We went just in time because the army began to kill newborn boys around Bethlehem. Mary and I have thought a lot about our son - we believe God has shown us he is going to be someone special.

Thanks for your friendship,

Mary and Joseph (and baby Jesus)

Jesus.homelife/webpage@theMillennium

Family

- the son of Mary and Joseph; has a well-known cousin, a few months older than he is, called John the Baptist.

Early years
- normal childhood; father a carpenter in small town of Nazareth; probably helped father in workshop; went to the village synagogue school and learned the teachings in the Jewish writings.

Young teen
- aged twelve, got lost when in Jerusalem (over 100km from home) for the big annual festival of Passover; parents eventually found him learning from and talking to the wise religious teachers at the temple!

Travelling

- around age of 30 started his work of healing and speaking to people about God; travelled from place to place; from that time on, didn't really have a home base, but stayed with friends in the towns and villages he visited.

✓ Favourite stays

- staying with the sisters, Mary and Martha, in the village of Bethany.
- stopped off for a meal in Jericho, with a cheating tax collector called Zacchaeus.

✗ Scary stays

- didn't like to go back to his hometown, Nazareth, because some people there didn't understand Jesus and threatened to push him over a hillside ledge;
- near the end of his life, was thrown into prison.

School report

What did Jesus do that caused such a fuss? Here's a report on his early life. (Jesus would have gone to school at the local synagogue but he wouldn't have had a report quite like this!)

Report

Name: Jesus of Nazareth   **Date: 32 AD**

Geography
Good knowledge of roads in the area as he walks long distances between towns and villages. Knows about water transport too as he sometimes sails on Lake Galilee.

History
Great interest in the Jewish religious writings and knows all about leaders from the past, such as Abraham, David and Moses. He uses this knowledge to teach others how God wants people to live.

Religious Education
There's never been anyone better at this subject! He has serious discussions with senior religious leaders.

Science
Clearly understands how the world works. He knows how to repair sick and unhappy people. He is able to stop storms on Lake Galilee and he can even walk on water!

Social development
Jesus is good at getting along with people, although some are puzzled by him. Not everyone likes him. He has healed people who couldn't walk, those who couldn't see and who had awful skin diseases. He has also brought three people back to life, who had been pronounced dead.

Comment
Jesus is an outstanding person who changes lives wherever he goes. Jesus of Nazareth has a bright future ahead of him and will bring light to the world.

Jesus of Nazareth was only one of the names or titles of the man whose birth we are celebrating in the year 2000.

Jesus
or Joshua, a common name, meaning 'one who saves'.

JESUS OF NAZARETH
'...of Nazareth' was often added to identify him from others also called 'Jesus' who lived elsewhere. Jesus was brought up in Nazareth.

Jesus bar Joseph
'bar' means 'son of', so Jesus bar Joseph means 'Jesus, son of Joseph'.

Teacher
People often called him 'Teacher'. They had a lot of respect for his teaching. Jesus taught about God and how God wants us to live. He was a great storyteller.

Messiah/Christ
'Messiah' is a Hebrew word and 'Christ' is Greek, meaning 'the anointed one' or the person who has been chosen for a special task, like a king. People in the time of Jesus were expecting a king to be born who would do great things. Jesus was seen by some as this promised leader.

The longer Jesus was around, more people realised that, in some ways, he was no ordinary man. Some understood that God had sent his Son, Jesus, to the earth. Many said that the fact that Jesus came alive again was proof that he was God.

Son of God

STOP PRESS !

JESUS ARRESTED AND QUESTIONED

The chief priests, worried about the popularity of Jesus, have arrested him. These religious leaders accuse him of insulting God. But his friends say Jesus is the Son of God. There are rumours he may be sentenced to death.

JESUS DIES, SKY GOES BLACK

The shock decision to crucify Jesus, along with two common thieves, was carried out today. Jesus was nailed to a cross and finally died. The sky was black as he died. Soldiers stabbed his side with a sword to make sure he really was dead. His body is to be removed and taken to a tomb cut into the hillside.

JESUS NOT DEAD, FRIENDS DELIGHTED

The friends of Jesus, the man who was crucified three days ago, have made an extraordinary claim. They say that Jesus, who was certainly dead, is now alive again. Some people say they have even seen him and heard him speak. Others say angels told them what had happened. The chief priests, who are now very worried, refuse to comment.

JESUS VANISHES TO HEAVEN

It is reported that Jesus, who has been seen alive by over 500 people, has gone to heaven. Before he vanished into a cloud, he spoke to his followers. He promised them the power to tell others about God. Already groups of his followers are planning to meet and pray together.

(m) Story times

Imagine a really good story: a great opening gets you interested. Plenty of mystery or excitement keeps you turning the pages right to the end. At last, you know what's happened. The end. What a let-down! It's finished, all over.

But the story of Jesus didn't finish when he went back to heaven. Quite the opposite. The followers of Jesus have a story that's already lasted 2000 years, and the story still goes on.

It began just after Jesus came alive again and the lights went on in the minds of his followers. Then the story went through awful times when to be known as a Christian could mean death by beating, hanging or, in Roman times, becoming lunch for the lions! (Since Jesus came alive again, Christians believe that death is not the end of everything.)

But the story has seen good times too. Hundreds and thousands of people have realised that Jesus can be with them too, to help make sense of their lives. Battles have been fought in the name of Christianity. Christians have disagreed over what are the right and the wrong things to believe. Yet the Christian faith has grown, spread over the whole world and is still spreading today. To find out how, read on!

It's great to be in teams, clubs, groups and gangs. What groups are you in? Guides? Scouts? Football team? The How-to-miss-PE club? One thing's for sure - you wouldn't bother getting together with others unless you thought it was worth it.

Crowding into a little room were the first believers in Jesus. They had seen Jesus after he'd come alive again. They'd seen him vanish into heaven. As they sat together, they planned what they would do and asked God to help them. Suddenly, something like flames landed on their heads. At that moment they received the power from God they needed and they set out to tell others.

Paul who was the first great Christian preacher, wasn't one of those first believers. In fact, he thought followers of Jesus were dangerous people who talked a load of rubbish. But then he heard Jesus talk to him. This changed his life. He travelled thousands of miles to tell people about Jesus.

Paul was put in jail, chained to the wall during an earthquake, shipwrecked and arrested. But he still spoke out about Jesus. Those who didn't like what he was saying thought the only way to silence him was to kill him. He was probably killed in Rome. Paul wrote lots of letters to Christians. You can read some of them in the Bible, like the letter to the Romans and one to a young Christian called Timothy.

Followers of Jesus started meeting together in groups, all over the place. They are the churches today (and we're not talking about a building!).

Dates and times

1   Calendars and diaries are really important to us. If we got the date wrong, we might miss the end of the school holidays and stay off school too long... (although that might not be such a disaster!)

2   But imagine missing birthdays and Christmas... (now that would be a disaster!)

3   Within 300 years of Jesus' birth, Christians, (followers of Jesus) had gone to live all over the Gulf area, much of Europe and parts of Africa. Jesus was having a real influence on the lives of many thousands of people.

4   But there was confusion about dates. In different parts of the world, people would arrive at places in the wrong month or even the wrong year!

5   So a monk called Dionysius decided, in 525 AD, to sort out the confusion and base all dates from the year of Jesus' birth. That is still the dating system used in most parts of the world! *

6   (It's worth noting that Dionysius probably got it wrong by four or five years!) But all years are now AD which is Latin for 'Anno Domini' and means 'In the year of our Lord (Jesus)'.

7   And dates before Jesus was born are known as BC, meaning 'Before Christ'. So...the year 2000 AD, marks 2000 years after Jesus was born.

*(In some parts of the world BCE (Before the Common Era) and CE (Common Era) are used instead of BC and AD.)

We might think we have a hard time... going to school, tidying our bedroom or walking the dog. But really we've got it so easy! There were times when people who believed in Jesus had it really bad!

Arguments broke out in 330 AD between Christians in Eastern Europe and those in Italy and the Gulf area. It was all over how to worship God and what to believe. Some Christians were still being put to death for saying what they believed. A number of greedy, money-grabbing church leaders were cheating ordinary people out of money and land.

In 1095, the Christian armies in Europe decided to attack the people of another religion who were living in the land where Jesus had lived. Most Christians would now say this was a dreadful thing to do. During four crusades, thousands of people on both sides were killed in battle... what a waste of life!

But despite all the unfairness, the battles, the confusion, the trouble and the arguments, the Christian Church just grew and grew and grew (like in the make-believe story of Jack's beanstalk)!

Changing Times

Seeing a page of words in a different language can look as though the cat has danced on the computer keyboard! If we can't understand the words, we can feel left out, as if they contain a secret that we're not allowed to know.

By 1400, most prayers and hymns were still in the ancient language of Latin. Ordinary people couldn't read them. They needed someone to tell them what it meant. There were just a few Bibles produced in English. They were handwritten. But 200 years later, Caxton made an astonishing invention. He invented machines to print books. Bibles could now be produced in large numbers. (By the way, Caxton was one of the six people nominated by the BBC as a personality of the Millennium!).

In 1525 William Tyndale became the 'father of the English Bible' when his English New Testament was published. He was arrested, strangled and burnt one year later. Then in 1611 King James allowed a version of the whole Bible to be printed and used in churches and homes. Prayers and other Christian books were also printed in English. At last some people could read the Bible for themselves and really understand it. It was like being let into a secret! As more people read the Bible, more people believed in Jesus and told others about him.

It is now very easy to find a Bible in English and one which can be easily understood by all people, including children. Parts or the whole Bible have been translated into 2211 other languages as well! To find out more, look up the last page of this book.

Over the last 200 years, people who believe in Jesus have been out to change the world! Jesus wanted sick people to

be cared for, poor people to be helped and children to be loved. Christians have tried - and still do try - to put Jesus' words into action. Here are some examples.

William Wilberforce hated slaves being shipped around the world. He worked to end the slave trade.

Mother Theresa saw the desperate needs of children living on the streets in India. She set up an amazing organisation to help these children.

Reproduced by kind permission of Mary Evans Picture Library.

Christians have often led the way to get rid of child labour, improve housing, and care for people, with organisations like CAFOD, Christian Aid and TEAR Fund.

Church buildings are all very different. Some are cheerful, busy places, others are pretty dull! Some are big, some are small. Some are very old, some are very modern. Many Christians meet in a home, a school or a community hall, not in a church building. And all Christians stand as signs pointing to heaven, remembering that baby born in a cowshed 2000 years ago.

2,000 years ago Jesus was born. 33 years later, he died. 3 days after that, he came back to life with a new sort of body. That means he's still alive today. He has had an amazing impact on the world. Christians believe that we can know him today.

So, that's what the Millennium is all about - don't miss it!

WHY CELEBRATE THE MILLENNIUM?

You have all heard about *Star Wars*. Such films are very popular nowadays. There are other films that are still popular, especially around Christmas time. These are films based on stories from the Bible. One of these - *Ben Hur* - shows horse racing as it was in Roman times. Four horses pulling small two wheeled chariots.

The Greatest Story ever Told is another of the Biblical films. This follows the life and death of Jesus Christ. Jesus is important enough even for the film industry to take notice of him.

You probably know by now that great importance is attached to the end of this year and the beginning of the next. 1999 turning to 2000. Not only do we change from one year to the next, from one century to the next but we change from one millennium to another. Have you heard about the 'millennium bug'? Computers crashing? It should be remembered that we number years and centuries from the fact that a particular child was born about two thousand years ago, Jesus Christ. He is the most important person ever to be born.

You have probably seen the letters BC and AD being used sometimes with dates. They stand for Before Christ and After Christ. AD is from the Latin, Anno Domini which means the Year of The Lord. Jesus changed our calendars, and he also changed our world. This is one reason why it is so important that you learn about him.

THE BEST SELLER

We learn about Jesus by reading the Bible. It contains 66 books - 39 in the Old Testament and 27 in the New Testament - written by various people and at various times. Three languages were used, Hebrew and Aramaic for the Old Testament and Greek for the New Testament. By today the Bible has been translated into many different languages.

Why is the Bible and therefore Jesus so important? The answer to this is that He has changed the lives of millions around the world. And this is still happening today.

A STORY TOLD

The New Testament begins with the Gospels - Matthew, Mark, Luke and John. This is where we learn about Jesus. The meaning of the word 'gospel' is 'good news', and the story of Jesus is good news. I mentioned *Star Wars* at the beginning - Matthew tells about a star appearing and leading the Wise Men to where Jesus was born in Bethlehem. Luke tells us about the shepherds leaving their flocks of sheep by night, and going to see what had happened at Bethlehem.

After the birth of Jesus his parents had to flee to Egypt with the baby Jesus. King Herod, a very cruel king, wanted to kill him. When you see people on TV fleeing from one country to another because people are so cruel to one another, remember that this has always been happening in the world. It happened to Jesus. When Herod had died, the family returned to Nazareth.

I am sure you like to know about pop stars, how they look, how they dress, what they eat and what their hobbies are. But we do not know such details about Jesus. The Gospel writers were not concerned with such matters. To them it was the life and work of Jesus that was of the utmost importance, especially his death and his resurrection. A large part of St. Mark's gospel concentrates on the last week of His life.

I am sure you do not like to be alone all the time - you like to be with others. It was the same with Jesus - he chose men to be with him and to help him. The first four he chose were ordinary fishermen on the Sea of Galilee.

When Jesus started his work he was very popular among the ordinary people. They saw that he welcomed the poor and people in all kinds of trouble. He also taught a particular way of life. When he was teaching he used stories about everyday life; he talked about shepherds and sheep, lost money, baking bread, the sowing and growing of corn. He won friends especially when he healed the sick.

It was not long though before the learned men of the temple became his enemies. At the time of Jesus the country of Palestine was ruled by the Romans and their leader (in Palestine) was a man called Pontius Pilate. The Jews, hoping to get rid of Jesus, persuaded Pilate to crucify him. Crucifying was the most cruel way used by the Romans to kill someone.

Do you like Easter eggs? The egg is a symbol of new life. Christians celebrate Easter to remind them that Jesus was not only crucified but that he rose from the grave. This is how new life has come to the world. Children sometimes paint eggs during the festival and these make the table look colourful.

BRAVE PEOPLE

The title of the book where we learn about these brave people is the Acts of the Apostles. It is found after the Gospels in the New Testament. We read of Peter being thrown into prison because he talked about Jesus. Then we are told about the first man to die for Jesus - Stephen. We call people like him 'martyrs'. He was killed by people throwing stones at him. A man called Saul took care of the clothes of those who threw the stones.

It is in the book of Acts that we find the word 'Christian' first used to describe a follower of Jesus. It was first used as a nickname in a city called Antioch. What about learning two Greek words? The word for Christ is *Christos,* so the followers of Christ were called *Christianoi.*

A MAN IN TROUBLE

The book of Acts mentions another important person. Do you remember a man called Saul at the time when Stephen was stoned? Saul was a Jew, and for a long time he thought he was doing what was best when he ill treated Christians, throwing them in prison, even killing them. He was on his way to the city of Damascus to do just this when he was completely changed by a dramatic experience. He was converted and became a Christian. Later he became known as the Apostle Paul.

From then on he travelled the countries of the Mediterranean to tell the story of Jesus. Think for a moment how we travel today. We can walk, ride a bike, go on a bus, train or aeroplane. It is easy to travel across the world. Paul had to walk or ride on an animal. To cross the seas, and he did this many times, he had to depend on the wind. There were only boats and sailing ships. His life was often in danger - he was the one who suffered now because he told the story of Jesus. The first thing that happened to him was that he had to escape from Damascus by being lowered down a wall in a basket. He was whipped, indeed he received 39 strokes 5 times; he was thrown into prison and on the way to Rome he was shipwrecked.

Look at a map to find the places where Paul has been working for Jesus. Important cities like Corinth, Athens, Philippi and Rome. He thought of visiting Spain but he failed to do this. Without a doubt he was the most important leader the church ever had.

THERE WERE NO COMPUTERS

Do you write letters to your friends? Or to thank someone for a gift? How do you do this? Paper and biro or pen? Or perhaps you have started using a computer and e-mail. Things were different when Paul was writing to the churches of the New Testament and to some of his friends. The same is true of the Gospels writers. They wrote on papyrus, a kind of paper made from particular reeds found on the banks of rivers. Or they wrote on animal skins. Skins would last longer. Ink was made from soot. You can see Paul's letters in the New Testament after the Book of Acts.

THE GOOD NEWS SPREADS

Remember we mentioned films at the beginning? The Biblical films show how cruel people can be. The Roman Emperors were called Caesars, perhaps you have heard of Julius Caesar. There were a number of these emperors. One of the most notorious was Nero. He is seen in the films eating and drinking, but he was famous for his foul temper. In his time Christians were thrown to the lions in the arena - to the enjoyment of Nero and the Roman citizens.

In spite of, or maybe because of, the suffering the Christians increased in number.

THE SUPERMAN OF THE ROMAN WORLD

Not exactly the Superman you know! The year 312 was a very important year in the history of Christianity. We have mentioned the cruel emperors. During this year the unexpected happened. A man called Constantine became Emperor. He not only became an Emperor but also a Christian. The history of Christianity changed practically overnight. Have you heard of Istanbul in present day Turkey? At one time it was called Constantinople in honour of Contstatine who moved there from Rome.

SO WE COME TO BRITAIN

No one knows how the gospel of Jesus came to Britain, and to Wales. The Romans came to Britain about 50 years before the birth of Christ. They made great changes, and were here for about 400 years. Maybe some of these soldiers were Christians.

If something really exciting happened to you, what would you do? Suppose you had a brand new shining bike, or a computer, you would probably want to tell your friends about it. And they would tell others. Something similar happened in the early days of Christianity. People who travelled, like merchants, or people who had been persecuted out of their own country, would tell others about Jesus. Some Christians somehow or other arrived in Britain and the news began to spread.

Can you draw a simple fish? The fish became an important symbol in Christianity. The Greek word for fish is ICHTHUS. So we have 'I' for Jesus; 'CH' for Christ'; 'TH' for God; 'U' for son; and 'S' for Saviour. The word for fish reads, 'Jesus Christ, Son of God, Saviour.' When two strangers met, if one was a Christian he would draw a simple fish in the dust. If the other was a Christian he would recognise the symbol, and they would both be happy. During the cruel times one had to be careful.

There is another symbol called the Chi-Rho. These again are the first two Greek letters of the name of Christ. The Greeks would write Chi like this - X. and R similar to our P. The early Christians wrote the letter P across the X, so we have the Chi-Rho symbol. This symbol was found on a wall of a house, dating from about the year 350, in southern England. This suggests that there were Christians in Britain at the time of the Romans.

ALBAN THE MARTYR

In Roman times there was a town in England called Verulamium. Here a Roman soldier by the name of Alban lived, sometime between the years 200 and 254. He decided to hide a priest who was escaping persecution. Alban was so impressed by the priest's prayers that he became a Christian. Soldiers were sent to look for the priest, but Alban took the priest's cloak from him and wore it himself. The soldiers took Alban away, thinking he was the priest. The judge was furious that the wrong man had been caught, and ordered that Alban should be beaten. But Alban refused to deny Christ, and in the end he was put to death.

Alban was probably the first Christian martyr in Britain. The town in the South of England is now called St. Albans, after the martyr.

WALES AND THE GOOD NEWS

You must learn two new terms now - the Age of The Saints and the Celtic Church or the Celtic Period. The Romans had left Britain around the year 410. New enemies, who were not Christians, came to England, and the Christians here already had to flee to Cornwall and to Wales. There was no Roman army to defend them. These new foes were the Anglo-Saxons who came from Scandinavia and Germany. The word 'Angles' has given us the modern word 'English'. This period is called the Age of The Saints and the Celtic Church.

In Wales there are many place names beginning with 'Llan'. This is the period when the 'Llannau' (more than one 'Llan') became important. At the beginning the 'llan' was an enclosed place used to bury the dead. Then a church was built. These 'llannau' were named after the saints, and this is why so many place names in Wales start with the prefix 'llan', for example, Llandeilo, Llanrwst.

This also is the period of the monasteries. The monastery was the place where a group of men went for peace and quiet to pray, worship and read the Bible. These men were called monks. It was the Celtic monasteries that kept the story of Jesus alive in the Anglo-Saxon period. It was an age of poverty and the monks worked hard to grow food and to help the poor.

One famous monastery was the one at Llanilltud Fawr, (Llanwit Major), in the Vale of Glamorgan. Here St. Illtud worked, and he became a well known teacher. He was interested in agriculture, and devised a new plough to cultivate the land. What would he say if he saw agriculture as it is today?

A PERIOD OF WAR

After the Anglo-Saxons a new enemy invaded Britain. You have probably heard about the *'Vikings'?* They came from Norway and Denmark. The meaning of the word 'Viking' is 'travel'. If you go to York you can visit an excellent museum showing the Vikings' way of life and their customs. They started coming to the east of England in the year 787. They also came to Wales. The Viking word for 'island' was 'holm'. So we have Skokholm off the Pembrokeshire coast. Remember too that the Viking gods - Tiw, Woden, Thor and Frigg - gave their names to the days of the week in English - Tuesday, Wednesday etc.

These Vikings were pagans, that is people who had never heard of Jesus Christ. They fought fierce battles against different Anglo-Saxon kings. They looked for anything that would increase their wealth. They stole valuables and treasures from many monasteries and churches. However, you should know that many of these Vikings did become Christians.

KING ALFRED THE GREAT

Alfred was born in 849. At four years of age he was blessed by the Pope in Rome. He became king in 871. He managed to conquer the Vikings in a battle in 878.

Alfred could neither read nor write until he was an adult. When he realised the benefit of education, he made plans not only to teach himself but his people also. He gathered scholars together to translate Christian books into the Anglo-Saxon language. He repaired the churches and built new ones. He made new laws based on the Ten Commandments and on the teachings of Jesus. He must have influenced Wales as well - one of the scholars who helped him was Aser from St. David's. He was the only English king to be called 'Great'.

THE CONQUEROR

Have you heard of the year 1066? One of the most important years in the history of England and Wales. This was the year when King Harold, the last of the Anglo-Saxon Kings, was killed by William, Duke of Normandy, (North-east France) at the Battle of Hastings. He was later known as William the Conqueror. Things were never the same afterwards.

Towns as we know them to-day go back to Norman times. The Normans were famous for using stone to build. They even brought stone masons from France to build here. Before this the building materials were earth and straw. This was the period when some of the castles that can be seen in Wales were built. But more important than anything, although the Normans were warriors, they were Christians. Their skill in building was used to build huge cathedrals, especially in England. They thought that large buildings would help people to worship and to live better lives.

MORE ABOUT MONASTERIES

If you go to Ewenni in the Vale of Glamorgan, South Wales, you will see the best example of a Norman church in Wales. If you go to St. David's, and visit the cathedral, you will see that the nave of the cathedral is of Norman pattern. The building of the present cathedral was started in 1181.

We cannot over-emphasise how important the monasteries were during the period from about the year 1000 to 1300. Apart from worshipping God, the monks did all kinds of every day work. They provided schools and hospitals. They also provided a place to stay for travellers, and there were many of them. Wales was a poor country in those days, and the monks provided the poor with food.

They also wrote and copied Christian books. In the beginning they followed rules laid down by St. Benedict. His followers were called Benedictines. But later orders of monks built their own abbeys and monasteries. There were the followers of St. Dominic, who were called Black Friars, because they wore black. Then there was the order of St. Francis. He loved nature and all animals. The Friars of St. Francis wore grey, so were called Grey Friars.

The history of the monasteries is rather sad from about 1300 onwards. Around the year 1402, a Welsh leader, called Owain Glyndŵr, destroyed many of the monasteries and abbeys. He robbed them of all the riches he could find. They recovered after this, but not to their old glory.

FAILING TO AGREE

I am sure you disagree sometimes - brothers and sisters quarrel, and you cannot agree with your friends when playing. Unfortunately the same thing happens with grown ups, even when they are Christians.

At the beginning there was only one Church. Rome became the important centre for this church. We have mentioned the monks and the monasteries. In the church there were other leaders called 'bishops'. As time went on the Bishop of Rome was given the title 'Pope.' You know there is still a Pope in Rome. One Church, one head.

But things changed in 1054. Think of the two cities, Rome and Constantinople. Rome was in the West and Constantinople in the East. They were in competition with one another so there was a problem - Where was the authority? This is an old problem which children know about. Who is the strongest? Who is boss? Who is most important?

A split happened. The church in the East was called either the Eastern Church or the Orthodox Church. This is strongest to-day in Greece and Russia. Its head is called a Patriarch. The Church of Rome is called The Roman Catholic Church with the Pope as its head.

A STRONG PROTEST

By the end of the fourteenth century, the church in Britain was the Roman Catholic Church with the Pope as head. From the years about 1350-1450 people began to argue how Christians should worship and behave. Some people began to ask whether the Pope and the Church of Rome were following Christ as they should. One of these people was a man called John Wycliffe, a teacher at Oxford. He was afraid that church leaders were more interested in getting rich than in worshipping God, and he was concerned that so many people were poor. He was also worried that people could not read the Bible, as it was in Latin. The priests of the Roman Catholic Church thought that they alone should read and teach the Bible.

Wycliffe, with help from others, translated the Bible - into the English language, of course. People could then judge for themselves how Jesus wanted them to live. It was years afterwards that the Bible was translated into Welsh.

THE PROTESTOR

But others were criticizing the Church too. To see the beginning of what we now know as the Protestant Movement we must go to Europe, especially to Germany. There, in Wittenberg, was a man called Martin Luther. He totally disagreed with the wealth of the church, with the way the church raised money and how it was spent. He also, like, Wycliffe, translated the Bible - into German, of course - as he wanted the ordinary people to be able to understand it. He composed a Book of Prayers as well as hymns.

You have seen posters displayed to draw attention to various happenings. Luther did something similar in 1517, when he wrote 95 reasons saying why he thought the church was at fault, and he nailed them to the door of his church. It was a traumatic event in the history of the Church of Jesus Christ. Things were never the same again in the history of the Church of Jesus Christ.

This is the start of what we call Protestantism. Note the word 'protest'. Followers of the new leaders were called 'Protestants' because they 'protested' against the methods of the Roman Catholic Church and wanted change. Luther had no intention of leaving the Church, but the result of his protest was that he was turned out of the Church altogether.

Catholic priests do not marry to this day. Luther had been a monk and so he was not married, but he changed his view and he himself later married. He began a new church called the Lutheran Church, the strongest church in Germany, and a strong Church in other parts of the world.

PROTESTING IN ENGLAND AND WALES

Here we must refer to one king in particular - Henry VIII (1491-1547). He married six times. The Pope in Rome was furious about this. Henry decided that he should be head of the English church, not the Pope in Rome. This is why 'Defender of the Faith' (what you see is F·D) is still printed on coins. By 1534 the Church in England had separated from the Church in Rome.

It was during the reign of HenryVIII that monasteries were closed again. One reason was that the king wanted the treasures of these monasteries. Many of them had become very rich.

After Henry VIII Queen Mary came to the throne. She wanted England and Wales to belong to the Church of Rome again, but after her came Elizabeth I and the country turned once again to be Protestant. This was when the Church of England or the Anglican Church came into being.

Even after England split from Rome there were still many who wanted to be Roman Catholics. Do you like Guy Fawkes night? This is to remember how, during the reign of James I, Guy Fawkes and other Catholics tried to blow up the House of Commons because Parliament sided with the Protestants.

Up until March 1st 1920 the Church of England was the recognised Church in Wales as well as in England with the Archbishop of Canterbury as its head, but on March 1st 1920, the Welsh church separated from England, and the Bishop of St. Asaph was made the first Archbishop of the Church in Wales as it is now called.

SO TO WALES AGAIN

The buildings of the Church in Wales, some of them very large, can be seen in every town and village. Have you heard a church bell on a Sunday announcing that the service is about to begin? If you go to some of these churches you will see beautiful stained glass windows. If you go to a service on a Sunday you will notice too that the priests wear robes, some of them very colourful. The colour depends on the time of year in the Church calendar.

Apart from the churches, you will also have noticed the many chapels in towns and villages. These are usually smaller than the churches though some of these can be massive. What is important in many of the chapels is the pulpit standing fairly high at the front of the building. This is because the chapels lay great stress on the preaching of the gospel.

One must remember also that chapels differ. The Church in Wales and many of the chapels baptise babies - but the Baptists do not. They believe that a person must decide for himself/herself to follow Christ before being baptised. Therefore young people or adults are the only ones that can be baptised. This is why they have been called Baptists.

There are other chapels which belong to the Congregationalists.

THE MAN FROM TREFECA

We have mentioned already how the conversion of Saul changed his whole life and outlook. In 1735 something similar happened to a man called Howell Harris at Trefeca, (which is in Powys today); and his experience changed the whole of Wales. This story is a very, very long one. The chapels belonging to the Presbyterian Church of Wales (or, as it was once known, the Calvinistic Methodist Church) started with what happened to Howell Harris. The reason for the term 'Calvinist' is that these chapels at the beginning followed the teaching of a man called John Calvin, a man of the same period as Martin Luther.

Apart from Howell Harris there were also other important Methodist leaders, men like Daniel Rowland of Llangeitho, who was a great preacher, and William Williams Pantycelyn, who was a great hymn writer. Another who composed hymns was Ann Griffiths of Dolwar Fach.

There are chapels belonging to the Methodist Church. These chapels were once called Wesleyan Chapels, because their members followed the teachings of John Wesley. This church started in England. The word 'Methodist' comes from the word 'method' - the Methodists were said to be 'methodical' in all they did.

OTHER WORKERS

It is most important to remember that there were many other people about whom one could write. For example, there was a man called Rhys Prichard, but known as the Vicar Prichard. He composed what we would probably call today the pop songs of the time. These were composed for people to learn about Jesus. Then there was a man called Griffith Jones from Llanddowror. He started schools so that children and adults could learn to read, so that they could read the Bible. It is ever so difficult probably for you to realise that the majority of the ordinary people could not read and write when Griffiths Jones began his schools in 1731.

Then there is Thomas Charles from Bala. He started the Sunday schools in 1795. Mary Jones walked the long miles to Bala to beg Thomas Charles to sell her a Bible.

TO CONCLUDE...

It is hoped that this short account has helped you to understand why Christians celebrate the Millennium. Remember that we live in a world today that is very different from any period that has been referred to in this account.

Do you go to a church or a chapel? Perhaps to a Sunday School? The title of the film *The Greatest Story Ever Told* is absolutely correct. The story of Jesus is the greatest and most important that the world ever heard and will ever hear.

H.Gareth Alban

SAINT DAVID

I wonder if there are people you admire? Perhaps you have an interest in sport and that you think of some personalities from the world of sport as ones to admire. Sometimes TV or film stars are our heroes. These are well known people not only to children but to grown ups as well.

But there is a different kind of person of whom every country is proud. You have probably heard of Mother Teresa - she worked hard to help the poor of India.

We in Wales also have people whom we admire greatly. You know that the first day of March is known as Saint David's Day. Welsh people, not only in Wales, but wherever they live across the world, celebrate this day. In days gone by children used to have a half-day holiday from school on this day. You would like that, wouldn't you?

We now refer to David as Saint David. However, when we seek information about his life we are faced by some problems. If you wanted to know more about any of the pop stars, such as Catatonia or Super Furry Animals, it would be fairly easy for you to find information and to be sure that it was correct information. But the situation is very different when we look at Saint David. In his time there were no printed books, films, TV or computers. People heard information by word of mouth. Naturally this meant that information could change or be lost altogether. So we do not know when David was born or when he died. On the other hand there are many, many interesting stories about him that have remained to this day, but we have no way of knowing whether they are true or not.

THE AGE OF THE SAINTS

Let us look briefly at the age David lived in. This year is 1999. If you go back 1499 years you are in the year 500. But we have to be careful with the dates when we go back a long way. We cannot speak about something happening in 500 in the same way as we speak of Manchester United winning three cups in 1999!

However, the period between about the year 400 and the year 700 has been called the Age of the Saints. Perhaps the most important period during this time was from about 500 to 570. When we think of the word 'saint' now we think of someone exceptionally good or holy, but in New Testament times any one who believed in Jesus Christ was called 'saint'. The Apostle Paul wrote to the saints at Corinth, but we know they were far from being what we think of as saints! There were many saints in Wales, men like Padarn, Teilo, Deiniol, Illtud and of course David. They are remembered in the many place names beginning with 'Llan'. Do you know of places called Llanbadarn, Llandeilo, Llanilltud and Llanddewi? Have you noticed, indeed, the many place names in Wales beginning with 'Llan'?

THE HISTORY OF DAVID

An important name for us now is the name Rhigyfarch or Rhygyfarch. He was the son of Sulien, the Archbishop of St. David's. It was he, some 500 years after the time of David, who was the first to write about him. He wrote in Latin, but his work was later translated into Welsh and called 'Buchedd Dewi' (*The Life of David*). But this is not the Welsh we know of to-day! It is called Middle Welsh. Many of the words are written differently. Take the word for 'to walk', which is 'cerdded'. In Middle Welsh it would have written as 'cerdet'.

Rhygyfarch tells us that David was the son of a nun called Non. Tradition tells us that she was a niece of King Arthur. According to one tradition his father's name was Sant, the son of Ceredig, king of Cardiganshire. Note the name Sant here, it is a proper name like John, not the same as 'saint' we mentioned earlier. Another tradition calls his father Sandde, who was a prince of Powys.

As I said earlier, though stories about David are plentiful and interesting, it is hard to know what is exactly true.

DAVID'S EDUCATION

David was probably educated in a place called Vetus Rubus. Rhygyfarch says that this place is 'called in Welsh Henllwynn.' But where is Henllwynn? No one knows for certain, but to the south of Aberaeron, in Cardiganshire, there is a place called 'Hen Fynyw', and I like to believe the tradition that says this was the place. But others think that it was a place not far from St. David - this also would make sense. His teacher was called Paulinus. There is a story about him going blind; none of his pupils could help him, so Paulinus turned to David. David replied that he had never looked in his teacher's eyes during the ten years that he had been with him. Paulinus was surprised, and asked David to place his hands on his eyes and bless him. This David did and his sight was restored.

LLANDDEWI BREFI

We must now notice another place in Cardiganshire called Llanddewi Brefi. Note the 'Llan', and the 'Dewi' (David). The Llan called after the saint. What about 'Brefi'? It probably refers to the name of a nearby brook.

The most well known story about David in this village is that of the ground rising beneath him. He was called upon to preach but because of the large crowd many could neither see nor hear him. But as he spoke the place he was standing on rose until David stood on higher ground where all could see and hear him. The previous speaker could not be heard at all.

There are many accounts of the miracles of David. He was called 'David the Waterman' because he lived on bread and water. But there are accounts of him turning water into wine, as well as resurrecting a young boy from the dead.

GLYN RHOSYN

The small city of St. David's lies in the South-West corner of Pembrokeshire. To-day you will see there St David's

Cathedral. It was here that St. David founded a monastery. In David's time it was called Glyn Rhosyn. (Literally *The Vale of the Rose*). Before establishing the monastery, according to tradition, David had to fight an Irish warrior by the name of Boia.

Life in monasteries in David's time was pretty hard. St. David's monastery was no exception. It has been mentioned already that David lived on bread and water. Study, prayer or work, taken in turns by different monks, continued around the clock. But they all had to be up early in the morning to work or to worship, and then they had to toil on the land for long hours. They were famous for their honey, as well as for growing vegetables, not only for their own use, but for visitors who often stayed at the monastery. They also took good care of the poor - there were plenty of them in those days.

David travelled to preach and teach about Jesus widely, but more especially in south-west Wales. He went on a pilgrimage to Jerusalem with Teilo and Padarn, and according to tradition was made an Archbishop there.

It has been said that David lived to be a 100 years old. The words reputed to have been said by him before his death / on his deathbed are amongst the most well known in the Welsh language:

'Lords, brothers and sisters, be glad, keep your faith and your belief, and do the small things that you heard me saying and doing.'

Rhigyfarch tells us that *'on the first day of March, Jesus Christ took Saint David's soul with great triumph, gladness and honour.'*

No wonder David was made the patron Saint of Wales, and that the first of March to this day is Saint David's day.

H.Gareth Alban

SAINTS

The stories about David, our patron Saint, are familiar to us. But did you know that there are many stories about other Saints too. On the following pages you will finds stories about Beuno, Cyndeyrn, Teilo, Cadog and Brynach. Enjoy them!

THE CAREFUL LITTLE MOUSE

When you come home from school and you're just about starving, what do you do? Run to the kitchen, I'm sure, and attack the crisps, biscuits and drinks. And if there's no food in the kitchen, it's not far to the corner shop or the supermarket to get plenty.

But it wasn't like that in the old days. Think for a moment what it was like for the Saints in the sixth century.. No supermarkets or shops, or even kitchens in some cases. At this time, famine was common, just like it is in the third world nowadays. The people were poor and money scarce. It wasn't easy to grow food. The weather was often bad, and at that time, there were no machines to treat the land. So one had to be very careful.

When Cadog was a pupil to Bachan, his teacher, it was a difficult period for everyone. There was great famine in the country, and everyone was suffering, from small children to adults. Really, many people were dying of starvation.

One day, after Cadog had been having some Latin lessons from his teacher he went back to his room in the monastery. Suddenly he heard a scratching noise. He looked around him and saw a little mouse carrying an ear of wheat in his mouth. Cadog tied a long, thin piece of string around the mouse's leg allowing it to run around. He played with the mouse for days. One minute he was running around his feet and the next was jumping onto his bed. During the night, when Cadog was asleep, the little mouse would go to sleep in the hole in the wall. But all the time the long, thin piece of string was around his leg. During the day when Cadog was in his lessons he would wander in the fields around the monastery. Cadog would often see him bringing a earn of wheat back to his room and disappear into the hole in the wall.

One day Cadog decided that he was going to find out just exactly where the little mouse lived. Perhaps there was a family of little mice. Maybe he was taking the wheat to his little family in the wall. Cadog dug and dug for hours, without finding anything. Of course, he didn't have much time as he had lessons with Bachan during the day, but by night he went on digging - deeper and deeper.

Then one night when he was hard at work, he dug through to a large room. Well, to be honest it wasn't a large room, but an enormous hall. There, in the enormous hall was a storeful of food. Cadog was so shocked that he ran to the monastery to tell the monks.

They decided to share the food among the monks and the poor people who lived in the area. Brychan the king heard of this. He was very impressed that Cadog and the other monks had shared the food with others. And thanks too to the little mouse with the long, thin piece of string around her leg.

CYNDEYRN AND THE COAL

Who? Have you ever heard of this Saint? Well, maybe not. But he was very important in the history of another Saint who gave Llanelwy, St Asaph in English, it's name.

Cyndeyrn was a Scot but he had to move from the country when it was attacked by a pagan prince. It was at this time that he came to Wales, and established a cell in the area that is today called Llanelwy.

Every day of the year Cyndeyrn would go to the river to wash. He would do this in summer and winter. One bitterly cold morning, after washing in the river, he came back to his cell. But he couldn't do anything, he was shivering so badly. He put some warm clothes on, but he was still shaking and shivering.

"I must get some help" he said, and he called on one of his favourite pupils.

"Asaph, will you come here for a minute".

Asaph ran to him, and Cyndeyrn said, "Listen, I have been washing in the river, and I can't for the life of me get warm, even though I've put warm clothes on. As you can see - I'm still shivering. Go and fetch a couple of pieces of coal from the grate in the kitchen . . ."

Before the teacher had finished his sentence, the pupil was on his way to the kitchen. When he got there he realised that he hadn't taken anything with him to hold the hot pieces of coal. The cooks in the kitchen started teasing and making fun of him.

"You silly fool, how are you going to carry them to the teacher?"

"I know," said one of the other cooks, "why don't you carry them in your hands, and then you'll burn!", and began to laugh hysterically. Then someone else had a better idea, "Why don't you carry them in your cloak and then maybe it will burn to cinders". The cooks were all having a fantastic time.

Asaph decided that he would carry the coal in his cloak. The cooks were positive that his cloak would burn. And there they were laughing and teasing.

Asaph carried the coal into the room before placing it on the earthen floor. Cyndeyrn thanked him for the favour, and Asaph said to him, "All the cooks were making fun of me, they were sure the coal would scorch or even burn my cloak. But look there isn't a mark on it. It's perfectly alright, not a scorch or burn mark on it."

"Go back to the cooks then, and show them your cloak." said Cyndeyrn.

Asaph went straight back to the kitchen and said to the cooks, "Look, my cloak is perfectly clean. There's not a trace of burning on it." The cooks were amazed.

"He must have taken it off" said one.

"Of course," said another, "the coal would certainly burn a hole in his cloak."

"No" said Asaph, "Cyndeyrn - my teacher, is a very special man, and has many extraordinary talents."

And he walked away leaving the cooks speechless.

THE PRETTY GIRL WHO WAS TURNED DOWN.

If I'm right you'd love to win the Lottery? A million pounds, maybe! What would you do with all that money? Buy a palace in the country, or a big family-size car, or lots of toys and books for yourself. It's difficult to imagine how much money a million pounds is.

This tale, tells of the son of a very rich family. They had plenty of money, and the son Brynach had everything he wanted as a child.

When Brynach was a young man, he decided that money wasn't everything, unlike his parents. He left home and went travelling around the country. He came across a pretty young girl. She was very fond of Brynach. Every day she would follow him around the country. But Brynach wasn't that fond of her. Although the girl tried every way to win Brynach's affection, he wasn't interested.

She was furious about this, and asked a gang of young men to catch him, dead or alive. The gang followed him to the river. It was there that Brynach spent most of his time. From time to time, he would see the occasional trout sliding over the stones. Another time he would see the dragon fly flying over the water. And other times he would watch the king-fisher diving into the water.

"There he is sitting on that rock", one of them said, "how about creeping up quietly behind him and pushing him into the water?"

"No" answered another, "let's stab him with the spear. One

hit and he'll be dead."

"That's a good idea", said another.

And that's what happened. One of the men went up to him and began talking to him, and another came and stabbed him in his back with the spear.

Brynach fell to the ground. The men ran away into the nearby forest. Brynach was in great pain. He called for help but no-one was around. He tried to get to his feet, but couldn't. Suddenly he heard the nearby sheep bleating. Maybe the shepherd was around feeding them. He called again for help. But nothing happened. The bleating was getting louder. In the distance he saw the shepherd crossing the field. He called again.

This time, the shepherd heard him, and ran towards the river. He pulled the spear out of Brynach's back and put some ointment, usually used on the sheep's skin, on the wound. He took him home to the monastery.

After he had recovered, Brynach began travelling again. By now he had decided to give his life to God. He established a monastery in the place where he had seen a white sow and some piglets. This place is called Nanhyfer. Not far away is Carningli, and it was here, so they say, that Brynach talked to the angels.

Brynach spent the rest of his life in the monastery, living his life for God.

This was the man who began his life as a very rich boy, but lived the rest of his life in poverty in the monastery. Brynach believed that living for God was more important than anything on the earth.

THE CURLEW OF YNYS LLANDDWYN

Do you enjoy going on a journey? These days, many people travel here and there, not only in Wales, but all over Europe. It is so easy to get from one place to another nowadays. Car, caravan, train, boat, and even by aeroplane. And it isn't long before you reach the end of your journey.

But it wasn't like that in the days of the saints. Although they roamed from country to country, the journey took a long time. Beuno used to stay in one place for a few weeks, and then move on to somewhere else. He often travelled through North Wales, from Gwyddelwern in the East, to Clynnog in the West.

One sunny day, when he had settled in Clynnog, he was looking over towards The Isle of Anglesey, and he thought to himelf how nice it would be to travel across the sea. The sun's rays were shining on the waves, and everywhere looked clear and settled. He walked slowly towards the sea with his small boat on his back. "It's a wonderful morning", he said, "I'm sure it'll be even more wonderful on Anglesey. I'll have a chance to look at the mountains."

When he arrived at Llanddwyn Island, on the western side of Anglesey, he had planned to write a little. He put his writing equipment safely in his cloak. He began on his journey. The sea was as smooth as glass. Above his head the seagulls squawked and the sandpipers whistled. Each one of them pleased that the weather was so nice. Beuno began to day-dream as he rowed along. The task of rowing was so effortless that day. He took a break and placed the oars at the bottom of the little boat. The boat moved backwards and forwards on the waves. Beuno bent over the side to feel the water. He bent over more and as he did his work fell into the water. He tried to pick it up, but the waves were carrying it further and further away. He picked up the oars and began to paddle, but the pages were floating ahead of him. As he rowed faster the waves also went faster and sent the pages further away from him. There was nothing for it but to sail towards Llanddwyn Island and leave the pages behind.

Above his head he could see a greyish bird with a long beak. It had been flying around the boat for quite a few minutes. Then he saw the bird plunge into the water and pick something up in his beak.

"Well" said Beuno, "that bird has caught a large fish. There he goes taking the fish to the shore to eat it."

By now the bird had gone out of sight and was flying towards Llanddwyn Island.

"I won't be long now", said Beuno as he rowed along, worrying about the pages he had lost.

A sudden wind came and pushed the boat along a bit faster. Before long he had reached Llanddwyn Island. He dragged the boat out of the water, and as he walked towards the rocks, he saw the greyish bird, the curlew, lifting the pages from the water and placing it on the beach.

Beuno thanked the bird, and asked God to keep it safe, forever. And that's why it's difficult to find a curlew's nest.

UNEXPECTED HELP

I'm sure you've heard stories about Saint Francis and the animals. According to the tales he had a very close relationship with the animals. But Francis wasn't their only friend, many others saints were too. One of these was Teilo, Sant David's cousin so they say. Teilo is associated with South East Wales.

It was a sunny evening and Teilo and his friends were out in the monastery gardens. For some days it had been raining regularly. But by now the rain had stopped and the sun was shining through the branches of the trees. Teilo was reading his Bible and praying. After reading for a short while he walked to the nearby orchard. He could smell the autumn air. Everywhere was quiet, only the sound of the crows squawking in the distance.

Teilo was walking leisurely from the orchard when one of the servants came up to him.

"There isn't enough firewood in the kitchen. So we haven't a fire to cook breakfast tommorrow morning. I wonder if one of you could go and cut some trees by the morning."

Teilo went at once, along with two others, to the forest to

cut trees.

When they had arrived they saw two deer walking nobely around the trees, one following the other. The deer came to them and started snorting and prancing gracefully around them. Then one of them began to rip the branches off the trees and put them on the ground. Then, the other started to do the same, and in no time they had enough firewood.

"Well" said Teilo, "I can't carry this load, it's far too heavy."

"We will have to carry them bit by bit" said one of the other monks.

As the monks picked up the wood bit by bit the two deer picked up the rest in their antlers and began walking around the forest.

"I know what we'll do", Teilo said, "I will walk in front of them towards the monastery."

And that's what happenned. The monks at the front, and the two deer following behind carrying the wood in their antlers.

It wasn't long before they reached the monastery. The other monks came out to see what was going on.

"What a funny sight" said one.

"Lazy monks - that's what I see." said another.

"We will certainly have a breakfast to remember." said another.

The little servant saw the scene and ran to the kitchen to tell the cooks that the firewood had arrived carried in the antlers of two deer. The cooks came out to see for themselves. The deer bent down and the monks began to unload the firewood and carry them to the kitchen, ready for the morning.

Teilo thanked the deer for their help. Then they pranced back in the direction of the forest.

Ever since then, when the monks needed firewood, Teilo would go to the forest to look for the deer. And without fail they would carry the firewood back to the monastery. As a reward Teilo would take a bag of wheat to them. Teilo and the deer became very good friends in the end.

THE BISHOP WILLIAM MORGAN AND HIS BIBLE

"Dad, what is that?"

Mr and Mrs Jones and their children, Manon and Rhys, were standing outside St Asaph Cathedral. They had been in the National Eisteddfod for a week, but now they had moved their caravan to a field near Llandudno, and today they were wandering around the area.

"A memorial to the translator" Mr Jones answered.

"What's a Memorial?"

"A statue to remember someone"

"And what's a translator?" was the next question.

"People who change things from one language to another." his mother answered this time. "These translated the Bible into Welsh."

"Why? "asked Manon.

"Well, the Bible is a very important book," her father said. "It tells us about what God has done in people's lives across the centuries - especially the people of Israel. At first people just told each other the stories, but as time went by some of them thought that they should write these stories down - in case they forgot the details. With time the stories grew into a collection of books. The word 'Bible' comes from the Greek word 'Biblia' meaning 'books', and there are many books in the Bible - law books, history, poetry, letters and much more."

"There are two sections in it too" added Mrs Jones "do you remember what they are?"

"The Old Testament and the New Testament" the children answered.

"Yes, Jesus was familiar with the Old Testament. It was written in Hebrew, the language of Israel."

"What about the New Testament?" asked Rhys.

"No that wasn't written in Hebrew, it was written in Greek."

"And it tells of Jesus Christ," Manon said, "Mrs Williams told us that in Sunday School."

"Yes, it does. Jesus friends liked to speak about him and that which he taught them. They told a lot about his resurrection. And when his friends began to die, other people started to write about him. That is what's in the Gospels - the work of Mathew, Mark, Luke and John.

"The letters that Paul, another friend of Jesus', wrote are also in the Bible" Mrs Jones added.

"He travelled a lot and established churches, and when he moved somewhere new, he would write a letter to them. That's what makes up most of the books in the New Testament."

"So, these men translated the Bible from Hebrew and Greek into Welsh," said Rhys looking at the statues.

"No," his father said, "I'm afraid the story's a little bit more complicated than that. Come and sit down here and I'll do my best to explain what happenned next."

After they had all sat down he said, "In time other people from more and more countries came to believe in Jesus Christ and they wanted to hear about him. But not everyone understood Hebrew and Greek, so people went on to translate the Bible into other languages. The most popular translation in Europe was Jerom's, a man from Italy. He translated the Bible into Latin. The name of that translation is 'Fwlgat' which means 'ordinary' or 'popular'. That's what the priests read from in the Churches."

"Did people in Wales understand Latin?" Manon asked.

"No" her mother answered. "The priest had to explain the reading to them, or they learnt it by looking at the pictures, in the manuscripts, and on the stained-glass windows and so on. In the end many people felt uncomfortable with this idea, and decided that they wanted a Bible in a language that they could understand. In England a man called John Wycliffe went on to do the work. In the fourteenth century he produced a Bible in English that everyone could understand, but the Welsh had to wait a few years until they had a Bible in Welsh."

"It was a man from Llansannan who campaigned to get it," said Mr Jones, "a man called William Salesbury. He went on to translate parts of the Bible that were read out in Communion Services to begin with, before publishing them in 1551 in a book called *Kynnifer Llith a Ban*. Then, with the help of Bishop Richard Davies and Thomas Huet - can you see them over there? - he translated the New Testament into Welsh in 1567."

"By now it was easier to produce lots of copies," added Mrs Jones, "before the monks used to copy the manuscripts and that was very slow work, but now there was a press company available and they could produce copies much faster."

"People were very pleased by now, I'm sure." said Rhys.

"Not quite" his father answered. "William Salesbury was a clever man, but his Welsh wasn't very easy to understand. It was another man's translation that became very popular. His Bible is the most famous of them all."

"Who was he?" asked Manon

"The Bishop William Morgan - a man who was born in Ty Mawr, Wybrnant, Penmachno, in the heart of the countryside. He was a clever child and was taught in the nearby Plas Gwydir. When he was twenty years old he went to St John's College, Cambridge where he gained many degrees. He came back to Wales and was a well-known priest in many places.. He realised that his parishiners needed a Bible that they could understand, and he went straight to work on one. He was a good scholar and he translated from the original languages. He worked on it for about ten to fifteen years, and he stayed with a friend in London for a year to make sure that the publishing company there produced it correctly.

His masterpiece appeared in 1588. William Morgan's Bible was an extremely big Bible. About a thousand copies were printed and they were kept, padlocked, in the churches, to ensure no-one stole them."

"And was William Morgan's Welsh easier to understand than William Salesbury's?" asked Rhys.

"Much easier" said Mrs Jones. "William Morgan's Welsh

was brilliant. As well as being an excellent scholar he was very familiar with the works of Welsh poets. He wrote the Bible in the finest Welsh - it was his Welsh that became standard Welsh in Wales. Some people even believe that it was William Morgan that saved the Welsh language from disappearing altogether."

"Quite a guy" said Rhys.

"Yes", his father said. "It's not surprising that he went on to be the Bishop of Llandaf and the Bishop of Llanelwy afterwards. He's buried in this very cathedral.

"But our Bibles aren't padlocked," Manon said. "So William Morgan's Bible isn't in our chapel."

"No, No" said her father. "Dr Richard Davies and Dr John Davies, Mallwyd did a lillle bit of tidying work on the Bible that was published in 1620 and then in 1630 came a smaller Bible, a Bible that people could have in their homes."

"But William Morgan's Bible was the basis for it all." Mrs Jones added. "That's what we read as children. Now there is another version too - Y Beibl Cymraeg Newydd (The New Welsh Bible). During this century many people believed that there should be a new Welsh translation. The scholars knew a lot more about the manuscripts now than what William Morgan did, and also many Welsh words had changed their meaning. So a group of learned people came together and in 1957 published the New Testament. In 1988 the complete Bible appeared, Y Beibl Cymraeg Newydd, four hundred years after William Morgan's Bible. It was presented to the Welsh in a special service in Cardiff on Saint David's Day.

"So William Morgan's Bible isn't used anymore!" said Rhys.

"Oh yes it is," said Mr Jones, "People still like the old translation, and very often - in a Christmas Service for example - they like to hear the version that has been familiar to them for so many years. We use both translations for different purposes."

"Let's go now," said Mrs Jones, "and take a look at the Memorial. There are carvings of all the people we have just mentioned around the pillar. Right, the first to see the most famous of them all - the Bishop William Morgan!"

MARY JONES AND HER BIBLE

Deep in the Welsh hills perched a neat greystone cottage surrounded by a patchwork garden of vegetables and flowers: green cabbages and orange marigolds, scarlet runner-bean flowers and purple clumps of herbs. The wooden shutters at each window, fastened in winter to keep out the icy winds, were flung open. The front door was open too, and summer sunshine poured onto the scrubbed stone floor of the porch. Everything looked calm and bright.

Everything, that is, except the little girl who suddenly catapulted out of the open doorway. You could see at once that she was in a bad mood. She stamped her foot and shouted something back into the cottage. Then, with a scowling face, she marched off behind the house, reappearing moments later holding up the corners of her white apron. Reaching into the apron she drew out a handful of something and flung it on the ground.

"Here you are, you stupid pecky things!" she shouted.

At once a dozen chickens appeared, scratching their way out of the bushes. Flinging out the corners of her apron, the girl emptied the rest of the grain over the hens in a flurry.

"I hate you, I hate you, I hate you," she muttered as the grain fell to the ground. Then she flounced off to the furthest corner of the garden and threw herself down under an apple tree.

The girl's name was Mary, and she lived about two hundred years ago on the very edge of a little Welsh village. Her family were quite poor, so she and her mother and father had to work very hard to make a living. Her father, Mr Jones, was a weaver. He would sit at his loom in the back room of the cottage all the daylight hours, whizzing the shuttle back and forth, to make cloth to sell at market or to the richer people round about.

Mary knew how hard he worked - and she did try to be helpful. But sometimes she just felt so miserable.

"It's so boring!" she would say to herself, angrily tearing

up handfuls of grass. "Everyday is the same as the one before."

Mary couldn't read or write, and there was no school for her to go to. So every day she had to help her mother clean the house and look after the garden. Every day they baked the bread and stirred the stew. Every evening they mended and patched their clothes. Every day Mary fed the hens. Every night she carefully locked them all up in the henhouse, for fear of foxes.

Most of the time Mary was happy: but she got tired of doing the same job over and over again - weeding the cabbage patch, when it seemed only a day since she had last done it! She would stand in the garden and look down the valley, wishing she had a friend to play with. For the Jones family rarely saw anyone else: their nearest neighbour was half a mile away.

But Sunday was their rest day. The big loom was silent, the house was spick and span, and Mary and her mother baked enough bread on Saturday to last over till Monday. On Sunday morning whatever the weather, the family set off over the hill to chapel.

It was two miles to the village, but Mary was used to walking and knew each step brought her nearer to her new friends - children of the other families who lived in the valley. They shouted and waved to each other outside the chapel, exchanging news at the top of their voices, until, all too soon, the grown-ups told them to quieten down and go into the meeting.

The service was always very long. Mary liked singing the hymns, but her heart would sink when the minister stood up to begin his sermon. His voice seemed to drone on for hours, and it was so difficult to understand what he was saying. The wooden pew seemed to get harder and harder, and it was all Mary could do not to fidget. If she did, her father would tap her on the knee and look sternly at her. To try to pass the time, Mary would count the cobwebs high up in the chapel ceiling, or make out shapes in the shadows cast by the chapel lamps.

But then suddenly, one Sunday, the minister said: "I have a very special announcement." He cleared his throat importantly. "We are to have a school in the village. All children may attend. The new school will open next week."

Mary could hardly believe what she heard!

When the day came for Mary to start school, she was so excited that she woke up while it was still dark. She lay staring out of her bedroom window at the black sky. She wondered what it would be like to read, to decipher the strange marks that held the secret of stories, of people and places she couldn't have imagined. Then suddenly she was afraid. Suppose it was too hard? Suppose she couldn't do it and the others laughed at her? Along with her excitement, she felt a tight knot of worry in her stomach.

So Mary was glad when dawn at last crept slowly over the hills. She jumped out of bed, quickly put on the clean clothes she had laid out the night before, and crept downstairs. She cut some bread and cheese for lunch and wrapped it carefully in a square cloth. Then she woke her parents, said goodbye to them, and set off to walk the two miles to school.

When she arrived, most of the other children were already waiting excitedly outside the chapel. At last Mr Ellis, the teacher, opened the door. They all filed in and sat down. The children were all together in one class, whether they were six or thirteen, because none of them had ever been to school before.

Mr Ellis handed out slates and sticks of chalk, and showed them how to draw letter shapes. The chalk made a horrible squeaky noise on the slate, but Mary scarcely noticed, concentrating hard, poking out the tip of the tongue with the effort. She had never enjoyed herself so much!

Mary learned quickly, and could soon read a whole page at a time. She loved reading the stories of Jesus and the long-ago adventures of people such as Noah and Jonah. One day, on the long walk home from school, Mary found herself wondering what it would be like to have a book of her own.

Suddenly she had an idea! She rushed home and burst in on her parents.

"I've decided. I'm going to save up for a Bible of my own!"

There was no answer. She looked at her mother and father. Instead of being pleased, they seemed worried.

"But books are so expensive," said her mother at last.

"More that people like us can afford. I wouldn't want you to be disappointed."

"Don't you start getting above yourself now, girl," added her father.

Mary was upset.

"I *will* do it!" she shouted. "If I have to save up for twenty years. Anyway, I *can* read. You wait till next Sunday; you'll see!"

She burst into tears and marched up to her bedroom. Her parents looked miserably at each other. Later that evening, Mary's father went to his workshop, and by the light of the candle, made a strong wooden box. When it was finished, he hid it under his workbench.

What a surprise for Mary's mother and father at chapel next Sunday! The minister announced: "Our lesson this morning will be read by Mary Jones."

With pink cheeks and pounding heart, Mary stood up and walked to the lectern. She carefully turned over the pages of the great book till she came to the place that Mr Ellis had marked for her. Then she took a deep breath and started to read. At first her voice was a bit shaky, but it soon became louder and stronger as she read in Welsh:

"Jesus said 'Everyone who comes to me and hears what I say and acts upon it - I will show you what he is like. He is like a man, who, building his house, dug deep and laid the foundations on rock. When the flood came, the river burst upon that house, but could not shift it, because it had been soundly built.'"

When she had finished, Mary hurried back to her place.

She shot a sideways look at her parents, who were beaming with pride. After the service, all sorts of people came up to Mary to congratulate her on learning to read so quickly.

"You must be very proud of her," Mrs Evans from the big farm said to Mary's mother.

"Well, yes, we are," said her mother. "But she has this grand idea of saving up to buy a Welsh Bible of her own."

"And so she shall"! cried Mrs Evans. "A girl with the determination to learn to read so quickly will surely succeed at anything she put her mind to. In the meantime, she must come and practise reading our Bible at the farmhouse."

So the very next Saturday found Mary knocking a bit nervously on the big front door of the Evans' farmhouse. It was a much grander house than Mary's. It had lots of windows at the front, and a huge yard.

Mrs Evans showed Mary into a room with heavy, dark furniture and lace table-cloths. There wasn't just *one*, but a whole row of books lined up on a shelf. Mary wondered what they could all be. Mrs Evans lifted down the Bible and pulled up a chair for Mary.

"Take as long as you like, dear," she said. "Then come to the kitchen for a drink before you leave."

Mary turned the pages carefully. She started with the chapters they had learned in school, running her finger under the words as she read. Then she turned to the very front of the Bible and read the story of how the world began. She tried to remember everything she read, so that she could repeat it to her parents when she got home.

After a while, it began to get dark. Mary did not like to ask Mrs Evans for a candle. So she lifted the Bible carefully back into its space on the shelf and found her way to the kitchen. Mrs Evans was baking at an enormous scrubbed table. She smiled and passed Mary a cup of milk and a warm welshcake.

"Come whenever you like," she said.

"Thank you very much," said Mary, and then added shyly: "What I'd really like to do is save up for a Bible of my own."

Mrs Evans smiled again. "I think you'll find your mother and father will help," she said.

Back home, Mary took off her cloak and hung it on the peg. As she turned back into the room, her father held something out towards her.

"We know how much you want a Bible," he said. "We'll all do all we can to help you. Here's a money-box to keep your savings in." He handed her the wooden box he had hidden under his workbench.

"You can have two chickens of your own, and sell their eggs," said her mother.

"And one of my hives shall be yours, so that you can sell the honey from the bees," added her father.

"Oh, thank you, thank you." Mary hugged them. "I'll work and work until I get my Bible."

And that is exactly what she did.

Children in those days didn't get pocket-money, so Mary had to find ways of earning the money, while still doing all her chores in the house. When there was any wool left over from her mother's knitting, Mary begged it to knit brightly-coloured socks that she could sell at the market. And when harvest-time came round, though she was very young, Mary went to work for nearby farmers, helping tie and stack the bundles of grain. But it was exhausting work, and she was paid only a few pennies a day.

Six whole years passed. Six long winters and six harvests. Mary saw six birthdays and six Christmases go by. She was now quite grown up - fifteen years old! But in all that time, however busy she was, Mary never let go her resolve one day to own a Bible of her very own.

Then, one winter's evening, she took down the box from the mantelpiece and tipped her pile of coins out onto the table. She counted and then counted again, just to be sure.

"Mother, father, guess what! I'm almost there! Only a few pence more, and I shall have enough money to buy my Bible! I can't wait for Sunday - I'll ask the minister how to get one. Then, as soon as I've saved that last bit, I'll be ready."

But Mary was in for a surprise. After chapel, she waited patiently for a chance to speak to the minister.

"Mr Hugh," she began. "You know that I've been saving up for a Bible..."

Mr Hugh held up his hand. "... A little bird told me that you have almost enough money now. Some of us in the village have taken a small collection to make up the amount you need."

He pressed a little bag of coins into her hand. Mary was overwhelmed. She knew that most of the village people could not really afford to give away any of their money.

"Please, please thank them all for me," she said. "Now - tell me where I have to go to get my Bible."

Mr Hugh looked serious now.

"Mary," he said. "The nearest place is Bala, and that is twenty-five miles away. Thirteen times as far as you walk to chapel!"

"I'm used to walking," said Mary simply.

Mr Hugh hesitated.

"But Mary, suppose when you arrive, there are no Bibles left?"

Mary turned her smiling eyes up to his.

"I know there will be", she said.

Mr Hugh returned her smile, but, inside, he wondered.

Mary's parents knew that, after she had been saving for so long, there was no way they would stop her going on her long journey. So, very early one morning, they hugged her and waved her off, praying that God would look after her. In her hand Mary held a knotted cloth full of bread and cheese to eat on the way. In her pocket was a purse full of the money she had saved. Over her shoulder hung a special leather bag which she had sewn to bring back her precious Bible in. And in her head she carried a name and address that the minister had given her. He had a friend who lived in Bala, and had told Mary that as soon as she arrived, she was to find Mr Edwards' house and he would be sure to help her.

When the sun was high in the sky, she guessed it was about

midday. She sat down by a stream to rest, drank some of the clear water, and rinsed her aching feet. She ate most of the bread and cheese, carefully saving some in case she needed it later.

After lunch, Mary set off again, but now the way seemed harder. The hill-paths seemed steeper, the ground stonier, and the sun even hotter than before. For the first time Mary began to wonder whether she would make it. She had already been walking for seven hours, and there was still a long way to go.

Then an awful thought struck her, sending a sick feeling to the pit of her stomach: supposing there was no Bible to be had? What if the few Bibles printed in her own language, Welsh, had all gone? Trying to push this thought to the back of her mind, Mary trudged on. But her legs were stiff and tired, and more than once she stumbled on the stony path, tears springing to her eyes from pain and exhaustion.

In front of her the path divided. Which way should she take? There was no time for mistakes, if she was to get to Bala before dark. Mary was afraid. She tried hard to recall the directions her father had given her. Then she chose the winding path that led up a wooded hill. When she rested on the stile at the top, she looked down and saw at last, to her delight, the town of Bala spread out before her.

From somewhere Mary seemed to find new energy. She practically flew down the grassy hillside to the edge of the town, and it seemed no time at all before she found her way to the house where Mr Edwards lived. As the door swung open, she suddenly felt shy. Her words came out all in a rush.

"Please sir, the minister at Abergynolwyn said you are a friend of his - my name is Mary Jones - and I have been saving up for six years to buy a Bible-and he said..."

"Hold on a minute," said a gentle voice. "Come inside and tell me from the beginning."

Mary looked up into the kind face of Mr Edwards and then followed him into the house. When he had heard all of

Mary's story, he was quite amazed.

"And you walked twenty-five miles just today?" he asked. Mary nodded. She was suddenly so tired she could barely stand up.

"Then first you need a meal and a good night's sleep. Tomorrow we shall see about getting your Bible."

Mr Edwards' maid led Mary away to the kitchen for a good dinner, and then tucked her up in a huge soft bed covered with a patchwork quilt. As her head touched the white pillow, Mary fell straight to sleep, dreaming of what tomorrow would bring.

Next morning Mr Edwards explained that they would need to call on a Mr Charles, who had received a parcel of Welsh Bibles from London, and would be able to sell one to Mary.

"I just hope he has some left," said Mr Edwards under his breath as they hurried through the narrow streets.

"You're very lucky," smiled Mr Charles when they explained why they had come. "This is the very last one."

He took out a beautifully-bound brand-new Bible and passed it to Mary. She took it in both hands and stared at it for a long moment. Her own Bible at last! She could hardly believe it. The she gave Mr Charles her purse full of money, and tucked the Bible safely into her leather bag.

"Read it carefully and learn from it," said Mr Charles as he waved goodbye.

"I will - and thank you!" called Mary, hurrying off up the street.

The journey home seemed so much shorter than the day before. Mary sped over the hillsides, clasping her leather bag. But she was very tired by the time she saw the lamplights of her own village in the distance. Her mother and father and all her friends were waiting at the edge of the village. Mary held the Bible high above her head.

"I got it! I got it!" she shouted. And to herself she added, "Now at last I can read my own Bible in my own language."

Long after Mary had left for home, Mr Charles sat in his study thinking about the girl who had saved for so long and walked so far to get a Welsh Bible of her own. Bibles in Welsh were in very short supply, and, even when they could be found, they were much too expensive for ordinary people to afford. Mr Charles made up his mind to do something about it.

And so a few months later, at a great meeting of important men and women in London, Mr Charles climbed onto the platform and said:-

"Ladies and gentlemen, I would like to tell you a true story about a little girl called Mary Jones..."

And all the people listened spellbound as he described how Mary had patiently saved her money and walked all the way to Bala to get the Bible she had dreamed of. When he had finished there was silence. Then suddenly people were scrambling to their feet.

"We must print more Welsh Bibles." cried one.

"And make them cheaper," shouted someone else.

And from a loud voice at the back: "Why not Bibles in every langage?"

So, there and then, a society was formed to make Bibles in every language for people all over the world.

Mr Charles would never have imagined that today, two hundred years later, that same organisation would still be at work. It is called the British and Foreign Bible Society. Together with Bible Societies in many other countries, it has translated the Bible into almost two thousand languages. So today almost anyone who wants to can now buy a Bible in their own language - without having to save for so long, or walk so far, as Mary Jones.

MELANGELL'S LITTLE LAMBS

"No, no, no! I won't"

Melangell's father wanted her to marry one of the Irish princes, but she refused every time. Although she was a princess she preferred to be out in the fresh air, not in a dark, old castle. The wild animals and birds were her best friends, and none of them were afraid to come to her. She hated it that all the princes enjoyed hunting these harmless, wild animals.

Poor Melangell. This time her father was determined that she would obey his wishes. So there was only one thing for it - and that was to escape from Ireland and travel by boat over to Wales to find a new home for herself. She landed in Gwynedd and walked east, and arrived at the Berwyn Mountains in Powys. She came across a beautiful, peaceful valley in the Pennant area, and there she decided to build a church. She wanted to thank God for saving her and for keeping her safe on her travels.

"This is a great place for me and for all the animals to live in peace. We will all be safe here." she thought to herself.

Unfortunately the princes of Wales were also very fond of hunting. One of these was called Brothwel Ysgithrog, the prince of Powys. One day he and his men were out fox hunting, but they hadn't seen one all day.

"I know what we'll do," one of them said. The prince looked very annoyed and he wanted to do his best to please him.

"What's that then?" Brochwel asked bluntly

"We'll go and hunt for a hare"

"What's the point in that? There's plenty of those all over the country."

"Yes, but they say that there is a white hare in the Pennant area"

"A white hare. That would be well worth hunting. Come on, let's go!"

The horses galloped up the valley, and soon enough the hunting dogs spotted a hare. Was it a white one? As soon as she heard them in the distance she began to run as fast as she could away from the hunting dogs. The men shouted and blew the horns, sending the horses on a wild chase and ordering the dogs onward. The poor little white hare! She was running for her life, but was too far away from her home to escape from the dogs. On and on she went, not knowing where to go. She heard the hunting party behind her, coming closer each time. She did her best to speed up, but she was beginning to feel very tired. She would have to give up the chase!

Melangell heard all the noise too. The sound of the horns and the horses hooves in the distance. Then the men shouting and the dogs howling. Oh no! she thought. Where men hunting harmless, wild animals here too, like they did in Ireland? And she thought she'd escaped from all that to a safe place.

Then she saw a flash of white coming towards her. She bent down and the little white hare jumped into her arms. As she held it close to her she felt it's little heart beating rapidly and his body shaking, but the hare knew he was safe at last. She sheltered happily under her friend's cloak, with no fear of the fierce dogs who were coming closer and closer. Then something very strange happenned. Every dog stopped still and went to lie down quietly in front of Melangell.

"What's the matter with the dogs? Sound the horn. Send them on!" shouted Brochwel. The horn-blower lifted the horn to his mouth and began to blow, but no sound came from it.

"Who is this girl?" the men asked one another. Brochwel was very furious by now, but the dogs refused to move any closer to the beautiful girl who was standing quietly in front of them.

"You've spoilt all the fun" said Brochwel to her angrily.

"It is no fun hunting harmless animals" Melangell answered.

"I own the land, so I also own all the animals" he replied.

"No, it is not you who owns the land or the animals," she said quietly. "God owns everything and he wants me to take care of all the creatures. Remember what Jesus Christ said:

'I am the good shepherd. As the father knows me and I know the Father, in the same way I know the sheep and they know me."

I also know all the animals and take care of them. This hare is like a little lamb to me and you cannot harm him"

Brochwel stood silent and shocked. This girl was very special and holy, for even the dogs obeyed her. He was sorry for being nasty to her and gave her a plot of land in Pennant where she could build her church. More than that he ordered that no one was to hunt animals in the valley ever again.

If you go to Pennant Melangell today you will see the beautiful church, and this story carved in wood. Before long Melangell became the patron saint of hares and in that area some people still refer to them as 'Melangell's little lambs'.

SAINT BEUNO AND THE CURLEW

Have you ever seen a curlew's nest? No?

Do you know how difficult it is to find one?

An old folk tale says that it is Saint Beuno who is responsible for this. Beuno lived in Clynnog Fawr and there is a large church in the village to remember him. A Monk and a Saint he travelled around the country teaching people about God.

One day he wanted to cross the sea to Llanddwyn Island to go and preach there. He walked down the beach where a fisherman was waiting him in his boat, ready to take him over to the island.

"The sea looks rough today" Beuno said as he climbed into the boat.

"Yes, but this old boat is strong enough to take us over safely," the fisherman said, looking over towards the island in the distance.

"I shall have to keep a tight hold of my book of sermons" Beuno said to himself, as he felt the waves pushing the boat higher and higher each time.

"Hold on," the fisherman shouted, rowing as hard as he could to stop the boat from going in every direction.

Beuno sat quietly at the front of the boat, gripping tight to his seat. Suddenly a huge wave threw the boat to one side. Beuno was thrown too and his book of sermons fell out of his hand and flew over the side of the boat.

"My book! My book!" he shouted, trying to reach over to save it. But the waves had carried his precious book to far. There was nothing he could do but stare at it, as it disappeared, and then appeared with the next wave.

"Everything I teach is in that little book," he said sadly. " I don't know how I will preach without it"

"I'll do my best to row towards it," said the fisherman, using all his strength to try and get the boat closer. But the sea was stronger than the fisherman and he couldn't do anything but stare either as it went further and further away.

Then suddenly a bird flew down from the sky, picked up the book in his claws and flew away.

"What type of bird was that?" Beuno asked excitedly.

"The curlew! He's stealing your book!"

The fisherman was really angry that the bird could do such a thing. Beuno watched the curlew and a smile came to his face.

"No, the kind bird is saving my book," he said happily, "He's not stealing it. Look, he's landed on that big rock over there."

"Oh yes. And he's putting the book down safely on the rock. I've never seen such a thing".

The fisherman was amazed, but Beuno wasn't. He knew very well that God had sent the curlew to help him. He looked up to watch the bird fly away.

"Thank you" he shouted after him. Then as the boat neared the rock, he leaned over the side and reached for the book. When he had hold of it safely, he kneeled down in the bottom of the boat.

"Thank you God," he prayed, "for sending this bird to help me. Bless all the curlews and keep them safe from any danger, like he kept my book safe today."

And that's why, so they say, it is so difficult to find a curlew's nest.

A Prayer for the Millennium

Heavenly Father,
Thank you for sending Jesus, your son,
into our world two thousand years ago
and for the wonderful story
of all that he did.

Thank you for the people
who over the years
have loved and followed Jesus
and whose stories are an example to us.

Help us today
to allow him to weave his love
into the story of our lives.

Amen.

Elfed ap Nefydd Roberts.

"LET THE CHILDREN COME TO ME"

Caryl Parry Jones

I remember very well standing at the front of Bethania Chapel, Ffynnongroyw and saying the famous verse:
"Let the children come to me, and do not stop them, because the Kingdom of Heaven belongs to such as these."

I must admit that I said the same verse in many other chapels since, but, perhaps because I am a mother to four children by now, the verse means much more to me.

It touches on two things; to begin with, it talks of the innocent mind of a child, and so little harm there is in that mind. Perhaps this is what Jesus had in mind, perhaps for us never to forget this innocence which was a part of all of us at one time.

But secondly, the 'do not stop them' reminds us that we shouldn't prevent their youthful spirit and nature. How many times have we heard adults complaining about 'the youth of today', forgetting that adults in their day used to say the same about them!

It is obvious that the ideas and expectations of our children and young people shape our future and it would be wrong to smother that spirit . . . "do not stop them".

"GRANDMA WENT TO BETHLEHEM"

Mici Plwm

Without a doubt my favourite Bible story is the 'Christmas Story'. Over the years like millions of children all over the world, who are celebrating the Millenium this year, I have, as a child, had the pleasure of acting one of the characters of this drama. Yes, I've been one of the flock; a shepherd, and also one of Herod's soldiers!

It is important to remember that each one of the characters in the nativity drama are important, even 2000 years after the event.

During this unique and important year - The Millenium, whilst looking in a second-hand bookshop I came across a colourful little book re-telling a small part of the nativity; and here it is:

Two thousand years ago in a country very far away from Wales, a baby was born in a stable. The baby's mother was called Mary . . .

But everyone knows this story already. But not everyone knows that is wasn't just the Shepherds and the Three Wise Men that visited that night.

Rushing towards the stable in their horse and cart was Mary's mother and father, that is Jesus' Grandma and Grandpa. There was no way that Reuben, their pet dog, was staying at home, so he had come on the journey too. He was an old dog - all hairy and rough looking, and although he was a bit smelly, they were very fond of him.

Reuben had lived with the family since Mary was a little girl.

He didn't know there was something special going to happen.

Something was attracting him to the stable in Bethlehem, and according to Mary's father there was no stopping him from travelling there.

"And a good job too" said Mary's mother as she looked around the stable.

"Joseph, whatever were you thinking of bringing Mary to such a place, and the baby about to be born?"

"Goodness me - is that a cow over there?" she continued

"And who on earth are these old men? And where did that donkey come from? I've never seen such a thing, never!"

"Don't lose your temper, keep your voice down" said Mary's father.

"Come and see the baby. He's really cute, and the image of our Mary"

"OK, lets go and have a look" said Mary's mother.

"Oh Mary, isn't he a little darling?"

"He's got your eyes, that's for sure"

"Who's Grandma's little boy then?"

Whilst Grandma was having a look at the baby, Reuben and the Three Wise Men had not been getting on very well at all! To be honest they didn't really like Reuben either!

All Reuben had done since arriving at the stable was bark and growl at the three of them.

Reuben had grabbed hold of the elder of the wise men's cloaks with his teeth, until it ripped. One of them tried to give him a sly kick, Grandma noticed, but not in time.

"There we go" she said, clapping her hands to try and get some order.

"Thank you for these lovely presents; but you should go home now, Mary needs to rest."

And they agreed without saying a word!

"There was nothing wise about those presents they brought for the baby" said Grandma, shutting the door behind them.

"Grandad and I thought it might be a good idea to get you a

pram"

"Joseph, I think that donkey and the cow would be more suited outside the stable; don't you?" Grandma told him, rather than asked him!

Without a doubt Joseph was pleased to see his mother-in-law and agreed immediately!

"OK Grandma, whatever you say"

This pleased Grandma very much, and she turned to the baby with a smile on her face and began to tickle him gently.

"Look Grandad" she said "he's pleased to see us. And I'm not suprised with all the strangers about this morning"

"Now then Mary, my love, about this lamb. The shepherds were very kind bringing it here, but it will grow up to be a sheep and then where will you keep it?"

"We'll have the same hassle as we had with the hamster, I'm sure"

"Listen" Grandma said to the shepherds, as she held the door open for them to leave. "It would be much better if you took this lamb back with you where it belongs, alright."

Mary and Joseph didn't look very happy . . .

"I know what we could do" Grandad said.

"This lamb could share a stable with our horse, and then Jesus could play with him when he comes on his holidays"

"Oh alright then!" said Grandma "but remember, you're looking after it - not me"

Grandma sat beside Mary . . .

"Well Mary" she said "I must admit I was very worried, and wanted everything to be perfect for our first grandchild. But to tell the truth its all very nice. Just the family at last"

"Reuben! Leave that lamb alone!"

"Strange too"Grandma added . . .

"He doesn't usually like babies, but he seems to be quite fond of our Jesus"

"Don't the stars look lovely tonight" she said

"It's as if they are shining especially for Jesus"

"Oh listen to me, silly old Grandma!"

"And goodnight Jesus - my special little boy" said Grandma "God bless you"

THE TALE OF THE LOST THINGS

Angharad Tomos

Do you remember ever being lost? If you can, do you remember how pleased you were when you were found? If you're anything like me, you're forever losing things, and I'm so pleased when I finally find them. I worry so much until I get them back, and then I'm happy again.

There is a story about being lost and found in Luke 15 (verses 3 to 10), the Story of the Lost Sheep. Jesus telling a parable about how the shepherd had a hundred sheep and he lost one. He wasn't satisfied with the ninety-nine left and he had to find the one that had gone missing. He left the rest and went to find it. He looked and looked until he did, and when he'd found it he put the sheep on his shoulders and everyone was happy when he arrived home with it.

Then we have the story of the lost coin. There was a lady with ten silver coins and she lost one. She wasn't comforted by the fact that she had nine left, she had to find the one that had gone missing. She was so worried, she lit a candle, and swept all through the house, and she never gave up until she found it. When she did she was really happy!

After telling this parable, Jesus shows us that God is like the Shepherd, and like the lady who lost the coin. He looks thoroughly for us, and is not satisfied until he's found us. Perhaps sometimes we feel so bad and so worthless that we feel God doesn't care about us at all, and that he doesn't want to know us. Maybe we move far away from him thinking he will forget about us. Then, we are like the sheep and the coin - lost, and unable to do anything to help ourselves.

At times like this, it is comforting to know that God is like the shepherd and the lady who lost the coin. He will keep on calling our name, and sweeping the world until he finds us. When he has found us, and when we accept him, there is much happiness in heaven. When times are hard, we shouldn't be afraid to say sorry to God, because we will be welcomed with open arms.

THE PRODIGAL SON

T Llew Jones

One day Jesus was teaching the people about God's love. To show them that God still loves them, even when they turn their back on him, he told them this story.

Once upon a time there was a father who had two sons. The father was a rich farmer - and lived in a lovely house. He had lots of land, cows and sheep, and many servants working for him in the fields.

The farmer loved his two sons very much, and although they lived a comfortable life, and had everything to make them happy, they were unkind to one another. They often argued, and one would be blaming the other for something all the time.

The father felt very unhappy to see this, but he never said a word. Then, one day the younger of the sons came to him, and said:

"Father I'm not happy at all. I'm tired of living on this farm. I want to go to another country far away to make my fortune. So I would like my share of your riches"

"No!" said the father unhappily; "I want you to stay here

with us, and when I'm old you can share the whole lot between you and your brother."

But the boy wasn't going to listen. He was determined to leave home. After seeing this, his father went ahead with sharing the money between his two sons.

For the next few days the boy was very busy planning to go away. Then, when everything was ready, he jumped on the back of his horse and off he went. His father stood at the door watching his son go down the path leading to the main road. There he waited a long time, until his son and the horse became nothing in the distance. Then he went back into the house, feeling very sad that he had lost his dear son that day.

The boy went happily on his journey. The big wide world was ahead of him, and his pockets full of silver and gold. He wandered from place to place, staying for a while in some of the large towns along the way. Those towns were very grand places, and he spent a little of his money in every one. Without realising his gold and silver was going fewer and fewer. But he was having a good time. Nothing else mattered. While he had enough money he had many friends and he felt very happy. One day he arrived at a beautiful city and he decided to make his home there as a rich gentleman. Every night his friends would come over to his house and they would have a feast and drink. Oh, they were happy!

He woke up one morning and realised that all his money was gone! He had none of his father's riches left!

At first he couldn't believe it had all gone. Then he sat down and thought about it. He began to cry. There he was in a faraway country - a poor beggar without any money to even buy clothes for himself. Then, he felt a bit happier. Everything would be alright. His new friends would be sure to help him.

But, when they realised that all his money had gone, they shyed away from him - every one of them.

He had to sell all his expensive clothes, and in the end

had to go and look for work. But there was no work in the beautiful city for him. To make things worse, the country was in famine, and food and drink in short supply.

He wandered from place to place, and by know he was dressed in rags, and everyone thought he was a tramp.

But in the end he managed to get some work. But he wasn't pleased with his job; he looked after some pigs, and he received little pay for doing so; and all he had to eat was the pigs food!

Whilst in the fields looking after the pigs he remembered about his father and his home. Yes, he remembered about his father and how kind he had been to him.

"How are things at home with my father?" he wondered to himself. "I'm sure the youngest of my father's servants gets more wages and food than I do" He thought a lot about his home, and how it was so far away now. Suddenly he got up and said, "I'm going . . . back to my father and I'm going to say to him: father, I have been a very bad boy, and I am no longer worthy enough to be your son. But please give me a job on the farm - as a servant"

And he left the pigs and began to walk home to his father's house.

He spent a long time on his journey, and had very little to eat or drink. But at last he could see his home. By know he looked very much like a scarecrow in all his rags.

His father had often looked in the direction of the main road hoping that one day he might see his son returning home. He was looking in that direction that very morning, and he saw a tramp coming his way.

Suddenly, as the tramp got closer, he knew who it was. Somehow he knew it was his son, despite his long hair and his tattered clothes.

At once he ran with open arms to meet the boy. His son hid his face in shame, and he didn't want his father to hug him. But his father was speaking to him.

"My dear son. You've come home. I was beginning to think

I'd never see you again." Then the boy lifted his head and looked at his father

"Father, I have been a very bad boy. I no longer expect you to treat me as your son, but I would be grateful if I could work on the farm as a servant to you."

But his father didn't listen to him. Instead he took him by the hand and led him to the house. Then he called his servants and said to them:

"Look! My son has come home. Bring him the best clothes and dress him. Give him clean water to wash himself, and put some shoes on his feet. Place a gold ring on his finger. Then go - kill the best calf we have and arrange a big feast." Call the harpists and singers! We must be happy tonight, because my son, who went missing, has returned home. Once I thought he was dead, but, look at him, he's alive and well."

That night there was a big feast, and there was plenty to eat, and the big hall was all lit up.

The boy looked around him and felt truly happy for the first time since he had gone away. He smiled to himself, and said,

"I travelled far away from home searching for happiness. But after all that the best happiness was here all along - at home with my father."

THE GOOD SAMARITAN

Dafydd Iwan

It was a cold January evening, and the snow was low on the Snowdonia mountains. The wind blew through Llanberis Pass as the young boy bent over the handle-bars of his bike, ready to start down the hill towards Nant Peris. He was on his way back from his grand-mothers house in Capel Curig to his home in Caernarfon.

Suddenly, two men jumped out in the middle of the road in front of him and demanded him to stop. One grabbed him, dragged him off his bike, and then threw him against the wall. "Thanks for the bike, anyway" said the man, sneering, "now then what else have you got for us?"

"Nothing, I haven't got anything!" said the boy, holding his shoulder, which was really hurting after being thrown against the wall.

"We'll see about that!" the other man said, grabbing the boy by his hair. They ripped his coat and his shirt off, and went through his pockets in a rage, "You're right, nothing is nothing!" he shouted in his face.

"You deserve a smack for that!" the other added, and began to fist the boy cruelly. After several blows to the face, the boy fell unconcious to the ground.

"Come on!" shouted one of the thieves, "someone's coming, and it's time for us to disappear!" and they jumped over the wall and disappeared into the rocks, leaving the boy whimpering at the side of the road.

A car was making its way slowly through the storm. At the wheel was a well-known county councillor, on his way to an important meeting in Caernarfon. As it happened it was a meeting to decide on a ten million pound contract to widen the road through Llanberis Pass, which would make the journey easier and safer for everyone. As the lights of the car flickered on the body at the side of the road, the councillor slowed down, and opened his window to get a better look.

"Oh how awful! The poor thing!" he said, looking up at the huge rocks above his head, and the falling rain which had now turned into pouring, lashing hail. "I must hurry, or I will miss my meeting, and this road will be like this for ever, and everyone's lives in danger." He put his foot on the accelerator and hurried down the pass.

A few minutes later, another car came to site, one of the passengers was a Bishop on his way to a centenary celebration in one of the local churches. "Wait!" he said to the driver, as he saw something white at the side of the road. "Someone's hurt over there. Remind me to phone for an ambulance when we reach the village; carry on!" And the car continued on its journey.

As the Bishop's car disappeared into the distance, another cyclist was travelling against the storm; his dread-locked hair soaking, and his clothes torn and ragged. He was what they call a 'new age traveller', on his way to a rave in one of the old caves in the Nantlle Valley. He was relieved to see the down-hill slope ahead of him, and as he began to glide down it he noticed the boy lying at the side of the road, and stopped immediately. He jumped off his bike, and placed it against the wall, and went to the boy. He saw that the boy was badly hurt, and bitterly cold, and he felt really sorry for him. He took off his coat, and put it over the boy; he tore off some of his shirt and used it to cover the boy's bleeding wounds, and gave him a drink from the flask which he carried with him.

The boy began to come around a bit, and the traveller lifted him onto his bike, and lead the way safely through the wind and hail down the windy slope towards Nant Peris. On reaching the village, he found a bed and breakfast, and after persuading the owner, they settled there for the night. The traveller stayed by the side of the boy all night, making sure he was comfortable, and every now and then bringing him hot drinks. By the morning the boy was much better, and the traveller explained that he would pay the owner enough money so that the boy could stay there until he felt well enough to go home.

"What's your name?" asked the boy.

"Why do you want to know?" the traveller remarked.

"You saved my life, and I would like to be able to repay you one day".

"You don't need to know my name; call me your brother and your neighbour; that's enough", and with a wink and a smile, the traveller disappeared through the door.

THE UNGRATEFUL SON

Wynford Ellis Owen

Sam owned a company producing computer programmes, he had two sons Twm and Rhydian. Sam began his career working for Hanna Barbera in the USA, working on classics such as Tom and Jerry, Road Runner and Scobby Doo. He returned to Wales in the early eighties, and established a television company working on children's programmes, mainly for S4C, as well as inventing cartoons for computer games. With the large increase in computer sales during the eighties, and the call for more effective systems, Sam began to specialise, and his work became famous all over the world. There was much call for his cartoons in the advertising and marketing field, as well as for television, and the fashionable pop industry found that some of his cartoons helped them to draw attention to their goods and records, and especially their videos featuring famous stars. By now Sam was a millionnaire. But there was another side to the successful business man and brilliant cartoonist, Sam was also known for being a kind and fair employer, and every one had a good word to say about him. He was a Christian, and he respected and loved everyone, like he respected and loved God.

His two sons, Twm and Rhydian, also worked for the company, as deputy manager and junior producer; but one of them was unhappy. Rhydian did not appreciate anything he had. He belived that 'the grass was greener on the other side' so the saying goes, and that there was much more to life than working for his father from dusk till dawn - despite the good pay. Another thing was that he wanted to experiment with drugs and alcohol, like the heroes he had read about in the pop magazines, and taste a different life, one which was much more exciting. As the months formed into years, Rhydian grew up becoming more and more bitter about his wishes, until finally he held a grudge towards his father, and blamed him for not establishing his business in London, and also towards his brother, who he thought was a waste of space as he had little ambition in his life.

One day, he had had enough, and he went to his father and asked him for his share of the company - 4 million pounds worth. Sam knew that Rhydian had been unhappy for some time, but he always refused to discuss what was worrying him, so there was no point trying to persuade him to change his mind. And his father was wise enough to know that his son had to make his own life, his own mistakes, learning along the way how to live, however painful the consequences.

And that's the way it was, he caught the first train to London, bought a comfortable flat near Edgeware Road, and started to taste the type of life he had always wanted. He made new friends, many of them, and each one very pleased to be friends with such a generous guy. He got drunk in night-clubs, and became well-known in Soho, and he was invited to the best parties, where he tried cocaine - sucking the drug into his lungs through rolled up fifty pound notes, according to some tales! However soon enough fools get separated from their money! He had to sell his flat in order to pay for all the drugs - by now he was addicted to heroine, the most addictive of all illegal drugs; and his friends turned their backs on him. After all, who wants to know someone who throws up in public, and is constantly making a fool of himself, someone who was once rich? He lived in a Salvation Army Hostel for a while, before he was mugged and beaten up by a group of alcoholics who used to squat in an empty building nearby. He broke his jaw-bone in two places, and his nose, and was in hospital unconcious for quite a while. Then when he came around, he returned to live in hell on the cold streets of London. He used to beg outside the new National Opera House near Covent Garden, eating the left-over fruit and vegetables from the market, left there for the pig breeders to collect to feed to the pigs. He watched with jealousy as crowds gathered at night to hear fantastic performances by the likes of Sir Bryn Terfel and the Lady Charlotte Church. His face and, by now, his heart were bruised, and he knew that he didn't have much time left to live, because his liver was swollen due to all the alcohol and drugs he had misused, and there was no purpose to his life. Rhydian wasn't living anymore, he was just existing.

At the time, while he was walking painfully towards his usual stall near the Opera House, he saw one of his father's cartoons being shown on one of the famous big screens in Piccadily Circus. It was a simple cartoon, advertising some new chewing gum, showing a father and his son playing football, and the father congratulating his son on scoring a brilliant goal. At once, he realised what he was missing out on. He remembered his father coming to see him playing football on the school field years ago, and how he would shout every time he scored a goal, and how proud he was of him for doing so. Then he remembered how much love there was at home, and how his father always tried to give him and his brother the best, putting their care and well-being first - even if that did mean the occassional smack on the bottom! And that's when the strangest thing happenned. Rhydian saw himself as he was, a failure with no comfort, no hope and no friends in the world, and he knew that his father wouldn't treat the worst villain like he had been treated. And that's when he decided to learn from his mistake, and go home and ask his father to forgive him. He had suffered enough, and he knew he would have to swallow his pride, and ask for help. He expected that his father would treat him as one of his workers, or at least, ensure that he had a roof over his head. But the strangest thing was that he was prepared to ask for help.

Ever since Rhydian had left for London, Sam's life, back in Wales, hadn't been easy. He missed him, and spent many sleepless nights worrying about him. Sam knew Rhydian well and knew that he would get himself involved in some kind of trouble. He used to wake up in a sweat some nights, thinking that he'd heard a knock at the door bringing the news that Rhydian had been found dead in some cellar, almost unrecogniseable from being gnawed at by rats and all sorts. Instead of facing his nightmares, Sam preferred to lie awake all night, and of course, in time, his health suffered too. But he comforted himself that Rhydian would come home one day, having suffered enough - and that thought kept him from giving up and losing hope. That, and the fact that God would take care of Rhydian.

One night, his faith proved him right. He was staring through his electronic binoculars searching the horizon hoping to catch a glimpse of his son, when he saw him. He didn't look the same, but it was definately Rhydian; he was alive - but in a terrible state. He ran to meet him, and put his arms around him, and kissed him. And that's when Rhydian asked his father to forgive him. He told him everything that had happenned since he'd left home, and admitted that he no longer deserved to be considered his son anymore, but that he was anxious to make it up to him, and to everyone he had hurt, including his older brother, Twm. He admitted that he was an alcoholic and addicted to drugs, and he asked for help. Sam knew of a place called Rhoserchan, a treatment centre for alcoholics and drug addicts, near Seion Chapel,

Aberystwyth - he had received an invitation once to be one of their sponsors. Tommorrow, he could go there and be treated by people who knew how. But tonight, they would celebrate. When Twm, the eldest son, heard that Rhydian had come home, and that his father was arranging a huge party to celebrate, naturally, he was jealous. But when his father explained, how he had dreamed that Rhydian was dead and that they would never see him again, but tonight, miraculously, he had come home, Twm understood how his father felt, and he went on to help arrange the biggest and happiest party ever held in that part of Wales. And that night, everyone appreciated what they had, and thanked God that the once ungrateful son had come home.

It is like this, possibly, that Jesus would have told the story of the ungrateful son if he travelled about Wales today - the only difference between my story is that the father was a farmer in the original, and that it was to a far away country, and not London, that the son went. I chose this story, because there are many young people today, unfortunately, in the same situation as the ungrateful son. I was so myself. An alcoholic and a drug addict, like Rhydian, I came to my senses in Aberystwyth, on the 22nd July 1992 - but the journey home was just the same, and also the welcome and happiness I received from my father, and everyone who knew me, when I arrived home.

I chose this story because I want everyone to know one thing: if Rhydian and I can find a way out of this hopeless situation where one is dependent on alcohol and drugs, if the same happens to you, so can you. There is a way home, and it is never to late to start the journey. Remeber that; and I pray that you don't fall into the same pit as Rhydian and I, however we both, funnily enough, discovered through them everything which we had always hoped and dreamed about.

JESUS HELPING TO CATCH FISH
(John 21: 1-14)

Martyn Geraint

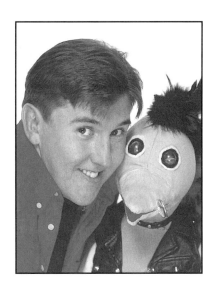

There are many stories in the Bible about fish and fishing - they remind me that I should perhaps eat more of them - but this story is very special.

It happens after the crucifixion and the resurrection. The disciples meet Jesus after he has ressurected and naturally they are very happy, but they have moved from Jerusalem to Lake Tiberius. Simon Peter decides to go fishing, and the others, including Thomas who couldn't at first believe that Jesus had resurrected, go with him. But that night they didn't catch a thing.

Early that morning Jesus arrived at the beach - but the disciples didn't recognise him. He calls out to them,

"Friends - have you not caught anything yet?"

"No" is the answer.

"Throw your net to the right and you'll find some". And sure enough they did, but there were so many fish that the net was too heavy to lift.

Then John, Jesus' favourite, said to Peter, "It's the Lord". As soon as Simon Peter heard this he put on his cloak and jumped into the water. The other disciples followed in the boat, dragging the net full of fish behind them - they were only about a hundred yards away from the shore. When they landed they saw a fire burning and fish cooking in the flames.

Then Jesus said to them "Bring me some of the fish you have just caught"

Simon Peter climbed out of the boat and pulled the net to the shore. It was full of fish - 153 in all, but the net hadn't broken at all. "Come and have breakfast" Jesus said to them. None of the disciples had to ask "Who are you?" - they knew it was the Lord. Jesus gave them some bread and some fish. This was the third time Jesus had appeared to the disciples after he had resurrected from the dead.

So why this story Martyn?

Well to be honest I could have chosen any story - there are many of them! But I wanted to chose an unusual story, one that is, perhaps, new to you, a story that tells you something new too.

I'm fascinated with the idea of miracles. Where something happens out of the ordinary, something exciting that makes you go "Wow!" afterwards - and fair play God has done quite a few over the years hasn't he?!"

Why fish?

As I said at the beginning there is much mention of fish in the Bible, for example the story about Jonah being swallowed by a big fish when he was trying to run away, and perhaps the most famous of them all is the story of feeding the 5,000 with only 5 loaves and 2 fish.

There is also a similar story to this in Luke 5. Once again the disciples have been fishing all night, and Jesus tells them to try again, but Simon Peter (who is very tired) isn't sure, but he tries again, and they catch so many fish that this time the net breaks. "Go away Lord, I'm a bad man!" he says. Jesus anwers "Don't worry, it is people you will catch from now on". After this event the crew stopped fishing and followed Jesus.

So what has happenned in between these two fishing trips?

Well Simon Peter and his fellow-disciples have spent three years with Jesus - this amazing guy who says amazing things and has done things even more amazing! They have seen Jesus welcomed as a King and then within a week being killed as an evil-doer. And during this time Simon Peter has turned his back on Jesus three times before feeling ever so guilty after hearing the cock crow.

But the disciples have seen Jesus again - somehow he has come alive again! And this has changed things!! Changed things for everyone - forever!!

OK - what's your point? What are you trying to say?

I want to say what's interesting about the story.

To begin with it's interesting that they still went fishing - I thought that they'd stopped going - but maybe they're trying to show that one has to work in order to earn a living and cannot rely on miracles every day!

Next - I think it's very interesting that no-one recognised Jesus, although they had seen him twice since he had ressurected, and he'd told them about this in the story in Luke 5 three years ago. To me that means that Jesus looked differently. And if he looked different to his friends when he appeared to them 2000 years ago - what's stopping him or any other spiritual creature from appearing in a different form now - there are stories about people meeting angels that look like real people - are these tales true? You decide.

Then - what about the miracle itself. Perhaps it was luck that there were fish on the other side of the boat, maybe Jesus had some sort of sonar detector that told him whereabout the fish were - some would call it a coincidence - a lot of coincidences happen when Jesus is around.

And what about the early breakfast? Does someone who

has come alive from the dead need food? I'm not sure, but people need food - and although Jesus, the Son of God, the Saviour of the world and the universe, can do anything, go anywhere and meet whoever he likes; he wants - and choses to prepare a simple breakfast for his friends on the beach. That includes Simon Peter - one of Jesus best friends who had recently turned his back on him. It's obvious that Jesus had forgiven his friend, rather than holding a grudge - there's a lesson there for us!

The End?

And that's it. A simple story about a fishing trip, that took place very early in the morning - or a story about the Son of God enjoying the company of his friends and encouraging them while on earth to fish for men - all this before he left them and returned to heaven to prepare a place for them and for us. You decide - I'm going for some "fish and chips!".

Bye for now!

THE GOOD SAMARITAN

Arfon Haines Davies

I wonder how many of you have heard of the wonderful stories of Robin Hood and his merry band of adventurers who lived in Sherwood Forest, much to the annoyance of the Sheriff of Nottingham. All their adventures sought to 'rob from the rich in order to give to the poor', and they would risk their lives in order to succeed in their worthy activities. Despite all the opposition of the Sheriff and his soldiers, imprisonment and the threat of death; Robin Hood and his men must have had God on their side, for they did succeed in their noble quest.

Then there was another adventure story which I loved, Dick Turpin the Highway man and his faithful horse Black Bess, and his famous ride to York. Dick like Robin sought to rob the rich to help the poor. Finally have you heard the story of Twm Sion Cati, a Welsh version of my two previous heroes? That is why I have chosen the story of the Good Samaritan because he tried to help someone who had fallen among thieves, and the unfortunate victim of their robbery had left him half dead by the roadside. Today we hear so much about a group of thugs attacking old people even in their homes, of physical abuse, and stealing a lifetimes savings in their eagerness to get money for their pleasures. It's so sad to know that the story told by Jesus nearly two thousand years ago is still happening not only on our city streets but also in country cottages and homes.

Violence to people and destruction of property has to be condemned as an abuse which cannot be allowed to happen, so we must try to be like the Good Samaritan.

He was not a popular man among some people, indeed there was a tendency to look down upon him just as we tend to look down upon the man with long hair, tattered jeans and not too fond of soap! It's so easy to judge others by their appearance, forgetting the old saying 'All that glitters is not gold!'

Jesus was the master storyteller, and he has six different people in this action packed story.

There is first of all the Jewish traveller, going on a trip to Jericho. He probably wanted to go for a swim in the famous 'Dead Sea', well known for the healing properties of that place. Unfortunately, this man was attacked by bandits, that's our second group of people, and they not only robbed him of all his holiday money but left him marked and bruised, lying half dead on the sand, an object of pity and concern.

Now two other characters appear on the stage of this moving drama, a Jewish priest hurrying along to take part in the service at the Temple in Jerusalem. He might have seen the unfortunate traveller by the wayside or perhaps he may not have seen him because he would be busy reading the psalm preparing himself for the important service which he would lead in the temple. Too busy praying and no time for the man in need. Then came the Jewish temple assistant, and he was involved in keeping order in the crowded temple, again too busy to see this poor bruised body by the roadside. We can all sympathize with these to people. They were too busy doing good that they did not see that there was another golden opportunity to do something special that day for a fellow man in need. Jesus wants us to realise that there are opportunities given to us to help each other on life's way.

Then comes the Samaritan. Not a popular person, the last person on earth you would think of, and he, this despised Samaritan, sees the man and feels pity for him and decides to do something about it, and that is compassion.

Kneeling beside him he attends to the wounds inflicted by the band of thugs, bandages him up and puts the man on his donkey, and walks behind him until they come to an inn where he nurses him through the night. Having to get up rather early the following morning, he pays the innkeeper, and goes on his journey towards the Dead Sea.

Imagine the surprise, and disappointment of the man who had been cruelly attacked, the following day, been told your benefactor had to leave early. What a wonderful person that Samaritan must have been, he even paid all the bills!

Of the different characters in the story, the unfortunate traveller, the creul bandits, the priest, the temple assistant, the Samaritan and the inkeeper . . . of all six, who would you like to have been, said Jesus? Those who listened to this wonderful story said - the Samaritan. He's our hero, he is certainly a Good Samaritan. Jesus tells the story to encourage all of us to be ready at all times to help make life better for so many people who need help in times of need.

This happened during the 2,000 years since Jesus told the story, and is a challenge to all of us as we prepare to celebrate the Millenium.

There was Francis of Assisi who was even known as a friend of the birds and all God's creatures, and Dr Barnado who took pity of the homeless children of London which Charles Dicken's wrote about in his novels.

Today we have people who look after others in nursing homes and hospices, not forgetting the millions of hungry homeless refugees of the Third World and even of Europe. Some people are preparing for the Millenium in the Jubilee

2000 project, which seeks to persuade our country to cancel the debt of the Third World to our country. Jesus said to those who listened 2000 years ago,

"Go and do good like the first Samaritan". Be a Samaritan in your Millenium Celebrations.

WOULD I UPSET MAM?

Roy Noble

Keeping something to yourself is a very difficult thing to do. Sometimes is can be exciting and you'll be bursting to tell someone, but you've promised that you wouldn't and that makes it very hard. Such secrets can be very pleasant, especially when they are meant to be a happy surprise for someone, such as a special birthday present or a planned visit as a treat.

Keeping something to yourself though, can also be very unpleasant and a great worry, especially if you know it will get you into trouble if the truth got out.

For instance, as a child you might have done something that you particularly did not want your parents to know about, so you kept quiet about it. I was once given a short piece of advice:

"Never do anything you wouldn't want your mother to know about".

We've all done it though; we've all been up to something that we'd prefer her not to know about, so our conscience will always remind us of that piece of wrong-doing.

Sometimes we do something without thinking. We don't mean any harm really, but there are other occassions when we deliberately hold back the truth and this is just one step from lying.

Jesus seemingly did something without telling his parents. Reading the Bible, the Gospel of Luke relates the one story we know about Jesus in the years between his birth and when he was a man. Little else is known of Jesus in these years. Luke tells the story of Jesus at the age of twelve going with His parents from Nazareth on their annual pilgrimage to Jerusalem for the Feast of the Passover. When Mary and Joseph began the caravan trip home, Jesus stayed behind without telling them. They thought He was in the throng of travellers and did not miss Him for a while. When they did, they returned to search for Him and found Him in the Temple, listening and questioning the teachers of the Torah. His parents were very annoyed with Him. He answered their sharp questions with,

"How is it that you sought me? Did you not know that I must be in my Father's house?"

However, you can still understand concern and annoyance. Jesus had disregarded their feelings and in many ways His movements had been a secret. He had kept the truth from His parents. However, if that was the only occassion He displeased His parents, then He could easily be forgiven for the lapse. His mind was clearly full of His need to be in the Temple and of His discussions. He didn't deliberately set out to delude his parents.

Many of us have many more lapses than we can remember with embarrassment and discomfort when we did deliberately deceive our parents to avoid trouble for ourselves. When I read that story of Jesus I am reminded of many things I've kept from my parents, some very pleasant and exciting, but others that caused me great discomfort and worry. One in particular comes to mind. Not only was it my secret in the end, but it really broke one of the Ten Commandments, number eight 'you shall not steal'.

I was just six years of age when it happened. It was during our annual holiday, staying with my grandparents who lived in Tenby. I loved going there because Tenby has many alleyways and secret places. My grandfather had two sailing dingies in the harbour, so it was an adventure playground for me.

On that fateful year, however, my mother had bought some presents for my cousins. She hadn't packed them and as the Friday of the week's holiday was a wet day I stayed in and secretly played with the gifts. One present was a plastic dog. His body was yellow and he had red ears and if you pushed his backside, he barked. The unthinkable happenned. I broke one of the dog's ears. I was in trouble and very worried about what my mother would say or do. I decided on a desperate move.

I took the plastic dog, put it under my jumper and walked back to the shop where she had bought it. I went in and quietly looked around. There were crowds in the shop and when I reached the counter where the dogs were sold I did something daring and dishonest. I looked around and when no-one was looking, I put the broken dog back on the counter and took the new one. Then I quietly walked out of the shop.

It was a terrible thing to do and I worried about it for years. In fact, I still break out in a sweat when I think of it now. I never told anyone. I kept it as my guilty secret.

They say that everyone lies many times a day. I'm sure if you think about it it's probably true. We all say white lies or maybe lies that protect others, but I'm not very good at it either. The discomfort shows in my eyes and movements apparently.

That incident with the plastic dog was a lie too, for my mother really thought it was the same dog. Not telling the truth or volunteering the truth, if that isn't the right thing to do, is the same as lying. You're withholding the truth. Furthermore, my secret was also theft, even though it was by a desperate little boy who was trying to avoid trouble. It's never worth it.

If you lie you have a good memory to remember what you said, and secrets, all secrets of that kind, will eventually get out. Keeping something to yourself can be very exciting, but you have to be careful of the dark secrets. They'll only cause you shame. To answer the question in the title, 'Would I upset Mam?', yes it would. Even if Mam doesn't find out, one person will always know. You'll know, and you won't forget it, ever.

CALEB
THE SPY

Maldwyn Thomas

Caleb was a happy boy in the Jewish camp. Caleb was Moses favourite. But Moses was very, very old. Moses had led the Jews for years, through fire and water. The Jews lived in danger. One night a lion had killed three of their sheep, and food was sparse. And then, a week ago, one of the Jewish shepherds had been bitten by a snake. The shepherd screamed and everyone in the camp heard him. And because they were afraid that the snake would bite them, the mothers took all the children into the tents. Moses cut off the bad flesh from the shepherds leg and sucked out all the poison and spat it on the ground. And the screaming stopped. But the shepherd died shortly afterwards. After that the camp was quiet.

But the people constantly complained. They whispered all day, and at night when they were sat around the campfire.

"It's Moses' fault" they said

"It's Moses' fault for leading us to this state of wilderness"

"We're tired of not having any food"

"Moses is always going on about reaching a new country that we can call our home."

"But when will that be?"

"Where will it be?"

The night before Moses and Caleb were sitting in front of the fire. Their fire was separate from all the other fires.

"The new country is very near to us Caleb. We're nearly there." Moses eyes were almost shut. But Caleb's eyes were bright.

"Are you sure about going on this journey Caleb. It will be dangerous."

"I am prepared to go. God wants me to go and see the new country. Those were your words."

"Perhaps I am to blame for sending you on such a dangerous journey."

"I will be fine."

Caleb was staring at the old white-haired man with his long beard, which looked like silver silk in the firelight.

"Remember you won't be alone. Joshua will be with you. And ten other men too."

"Do we have to have so many men? Two would be enough. One to keep a look-out, and one to spy."

"Spying. That's what you'll all be doing Caleb. Twelve spies going to see the new country."

The flames of the fire were quietly falling into the ashes.

"I'll make sure the work's done. You will hear what sort of country it is, and what the people who live there are like."

"Remember you are the youngest Caleb. And I am so old."

"You'll never be old. You're Moses. God's man. You have led us to the new country."

"God leads. It is God who wants you to know about this country; about the land - whether it's good farming land? Or is it thin and soily?"

"And we want to know about the people who live there too. If they are strong people, dangerous people."

"Those are the important questions Caleb."

"I'm itching to go. And Joshua's ready to go too. But I don't know about the other ten?"

"You stay close to Joshua. He's a good soldier."

"Joshua and his long knife," said Caleb.

"I'm going to be a soldier like Joshua in the new country."

"But remember Caleb we will need farmers there too. Soldiers to guard the country and farmers to make the country our home."

Caleb had been looking at the big city wall for hours. From dawn to dusk he stared at the city wall. By now it was nightime and the city people were asleep.

But every quarter of an hour soldiers walked up and down the city wall calling on one another. They walked along the wall all night. The soldiers guarded the city and its people. The wall looked massive in the starlight. The soldiers called to one another reporting that everything was alright. Caleb looked at the wall once again. He looked at all the stones, and at every crack and gap in between them. A cloud came over.

Caleb got up in the shadows. He ran in between the bushes at the foot of the wall. Then suddenly he was climbing. His hands in the cracks between the stones. His feet in the gaps. He was pulling himself up the wall, not daring to look down to the bushes below. Up and up the big wall.

Then he waited. Holding on to a stone and his feet in a gap. Quarter of an hour had gone. Caleb heard the soldiers calling one another above his head. Two minutes? A minute? They had to work quickly.

Caleb looked down at the city streets. There were stone buildings. And oil lamps in some of them. He could see through the door of one of them. There were soldiers sitting down and some standing. They were tall men. And their shadows on the wall made them looked like giants.

Then Caleb heard footsteps coming along the wall.

He climbed over the edge and grabbed hold of the stones. His hands were in the cracks between the stones and the top of the wall. Two soldiers stood directly above Caleb. Their long swords scratching the top of the wall above Caleb's shadow. His head was spinning. His hair dripping with sweat. His fingers were freezing. The soldiers were still talking above his head, and their swords scraped the floor as they chatted.

Caleb began to lower himself from stone to stone. From crack to crack. Down the wall. Why hadn't the soldiers looked over the wall and seen him? How come he was still alive, after lowering himself down the big wall? How did the soldiers not spot him in the starlight.

He landed in one of the bushes at the bottom of the wall. Another cloud came over the stars. He got up and ran through the bushes. In between shadows. Joshua was waiting for him in the sheep pen. The sheep were grazing happily. There was little noise apart from the occasional bleat and the noise of the sheep chewing.

"I was going to wait for another half and hour and that's all.. Why were you so long?" Joshua said holding his knife.

"Ssh, be quiet!"

"What's wrong Caleb?"

"Over there. Somebody's walking beside the hedge."

Joshua looked and could see someone on the other side of the pen.

Someone was walking towards them. The sheep became disturbed, and began to bleat louder and more often.

Joshua scoured the darkness.

"Where did he come from? I haven't seen anyone all day, nor tonight."

"You're the soldier Joshua. You're supposed to be on the look out."

And then they heard loud, pierce singing, and the sheep began to bleat even louder.

"It's a shepherd. He must be drunk. And must've been lying in the pen for hours sleeping it off."

"He's awake by now and walking towards us." The singing got louder and the bleating got louder. The sheep began to move around the pen.

Stars gave light. The person was pushing hard against the sheep. Caleb could see a large stick being lifted in the air.

"He will have woken everyone in the city," Caleb said, turning to Joshua. But Joshua was in the middle of the sheep. Caleb saw his long knife shining in the starlight.

"No, Joshua, don't!"

Caleb ran after him. But Joshua was face to face with the man.

"Don't! Don't Joshua!"

Caleb was too late.

He saw the long knife lifting quickly. Caleb threw himself to the floor of the pen. Soil, dirt, leaves. He closed his eyes, closed his ears. And Joshua's long knife was going up and down, in and out, and the sheep were bleating frantically.

"Come on Caleb, come on!"

Joshua was drying the blade of his long knife. But Caleb wasn't listening. He got up slowly and began to walk among the sheep. Walking backwards and forwards, along and across the pen. Joshua could hear the boy talking quietly, and the animals calmed. The wild bleating quietened. It was still quiet in the city too. Not one soldier was watching from the top of the wall. Caleb and Joshua left the pen quietly.

They walked all night until dawn. They reached a vineyard and a derelict building with no roof. There the ten spy's were hiding, they were asleep. They began to question:

"What did you see?"

"A big city. With walls as high as the clouds," answered Caleb

"And soldiers?"

"Huge soldiers. Each one like a giant."

"And were they armed?"

"They've got swords the size of the sun's rays," answered Caleb again.

"What hope have we got then? And why are you smiling Caleb?"

"I'm smiling because I'm happy. I have seen our new country."

"You're mad! Cities in the sky. Soldiers like giants. We've got no chance of winning the country."

"We will win the country because God is with us." replied Caleb, still smiling.

"God was with us when I was hanging from the top of the wall and the soldiers were standing right above my head. Nobody saw me although the starlight was lighting up the wall."

"Caleb's right" added Joshua.

"Come on, we've got some good news for Moses. God will be with us in the new country."

As they were walking out of the vineyard Caleb and Joshua cut off some bunches of grapes off the trees. They carried them on their shoulders.

"To show that the land is good," Joshua said over his shoulder to the ten that were following slowly behind them.

"I'm happy for another reason too," said Caleb to the soldier

"What's that then?"

"Last night has shown me the future. I know what we'll both be doing in a few years."

"Well?"

"You will be a famous soldier Joshua. You will lead us into the new country."

Joshua looked at the boy.

"And what will you be doing Caleb?"

"Farming. Shepherding. Taking care of the new land. And collecting the grapes every July."

The grapes shone in the sunlight, and they shared the carrying.

When they arrived back at the camp the sun was setting. Moses was standing waiting for them.

Caleb's story can be found in the books of Numbers and Joshua in the Bible.

THE ISLAND AND THE LACE GLOVES

In 1947 when I was about seven years old, I received a present through the post. Nothing unusual in that, I hear you say . . . but the parcel came from a faraway country, and throughout the second world war very few parcels had arrived in Wales from faraway countries.

It was a small, light parcel; I ripped off the brown paper and inside was a small pair of the prettiest gloves you have ever seen - white lace ones with lace trimmings around the wrists. Ladies today wouldn't wear them, but in the forties that's what you would wear on your hands during the summer to go to chapel. I loved my present, the gloves fitted perfectly and I always wore them every summer until they got too small.

But what was so special about the lace gloves? Two things I believe. They came from a big island called Madagascar, where women were famous for their works of lace; and secondly my great uncle who sent them to me had lived there for over 40 years as a missionary, with many other Welsh who lived and worked there since the beginning of the last century.

Since as far back as 1796 people from Wales had been collecting money for missionary work. Thomas Charles from Bala went to visit the ship *Duff* when it returned from the South Sea Islands. In Thomas Phillips' school in Neuadd-Lwyd, Cardiganshire, many students discovered their ambition to go and preach about Jesus Christ in faraway countries. **David Jones** was only sixteen when he began preaching in 1813. Another boy, about the same age, was **Thomas Bevan**. Both boys were very able, full of energy and they had decided early that they wanted to be preachers and missionaries. By 1817, after a short period of studying in England, they were both preparing to go to Madagascar with their young wives.

Today, to get to Madagascar we would fly in an aeroplane or cruise leisurely in a luxury ship along the Suez canal. In 1818 travelling to Madagascar meant many months onboard a fragile sailing ship travelling the west coast of Africa. How brave! But both families were full of hope and confidence and were looking forward to living on the island that was described as paradise, a country of forests and lakes and kind, welcoming people.

But their dreams were shattered within a few months of living there, for in August 1818 they were hit by a infectious disease and five of them died - Thomas Bevan, his wife and baby, and David Jones' wife and baby. David Jones was left there lonely, sad and weak, but he wasn't a person to give up easily. He battled on and before long in 1821 another Welshman came to join him - David Griffiths from Wynfe, Carmarthenshire. Whilst David Jones was a thin man, frail after the disease, David Griffiths was a big, strong man. The two became the best of friends and worked hard together. Besides learning to speak French and read Latin, Greek and Hebrew, the two also went at it to learn the language of Madagascar - Malgasi - fluently. They had the support of the king Radama who saw that the men wanted to help the people, and so he gave them a house each.

They both knew how important the Bible was to the people of Wales and they were determined to make it as treasured in Madagascar. But the language - Malagasi - wasn't a written language. So they began to write the language. The first problem was which alphabet to use to represent various sounds in the language. Welsh is more or less a phonetic language, where every sound has its own letter - different from English - and this makes it easier to read. So they decided to follow the same pattern as Welsh and have a letter for every sound. But John Jeffries, and English missionary who was with them, wasn't happy with this. There were many arguments between them and the London Missionary Society who supported Jeffries. They wanted English to be the basis for the Madagascar alphabet. But David Griffiths wasn't one to give in easily; he was a man who stood for what he belived in, a stubborn man according to his rivals. As he was sure that it was his and David Jones' decision that was the right one, he refused to give in, and Wales conquered. It was a difficult battle, but this was one of Wales biggest favours to Madagascar - ensuring a language that was easy to read.

The next step was to translate the Bible and also 'Taith y Pererin' (The Pilgrims Journey), two books that were in nearly every house in Wales during the last century. They also had to teach the people to read and write and so they established schools all over the island. Many children and young people, both boys and girls, came from all around to attend. David Griffiths said: "Our young pupils are so eager and thirsty for information that they are around the house every morning before the break of dawn asking for school." More company came over from Wales - David Johns from Llanina, Cardiganshire who helped to translate the Bible - three David's at it now!! By 1836 the Bible was ready in the language of Madagascar, and most of that due to the work of the missionaries from Wales.

But the same year the king Radama, the missionarie's friend, died and a difficult time began in the country under the reign of the queen Ranavalona, the 'nasty queen' as she was called afterwards. She wanted to go back to the pagan beliefs and she punished the christians cruelly. They were killed for merely holding a Bible. But although the missionaries had to escape, the people of Madagascar were faithful and brave; they hid and buried millions of Bibles and when Ranavalona died in 1861 the missionaries returned. This time it was a husband and wife from Pembrokeshire, Thomas and Elizabeth Rowlands, who helped to re-establish the churches in Madagascar, and after them many others came to keep the connection between Wales and Madagascar.

In 1910 my great uncle, Daniel Owen Jones went to Madagascar and preached and taught there for fourty years. He was a headmaster in the College of Divinity in the capital city of Antananarivo, and he translated many Welsh hymns, as the people of Madagascar were very fond of singing.

Many years after he had died another relative of mine visited Madagascar and on travelling around the southern area of the island he met a man outside a church who asked him where he came from. "From Wales" he answered and the man said "It was a Welshman by the name of Jones who taught me in college."

"Daniel Owen Jones was my cousin" answered my relative. Without saying a word the man ran into the church and returned with the Malagasi hymn book in his hand. "Here you are" he said, "D.O.Jones' work" pointing out the various hymns, among them 'Calon Lan' (a traditional Welsh hymn). So if you ever go to Madagascar you may hear 'Calon Lan' being sung by the millions who go to church there in every village and town - and you will feel quite at home. You will walk along David Jones Street and Thomas Bevan Street in the capital city Antananarivo, and feel very proud that a country so far away honours two Welshmen for helping the country out. In Trantovato Church in Toamasina there is a copy of the Welsh Bible in the altar and in Minny Street Church, Cardiff there is a copy of the Malagasgi Bible, because the churches have twinned. Yes, there is still a strong tie between Wales and Madagascar.

And yes . . . after all these years I still have the little lace gloves, the first thing to impulse me to work with Christian Aid today.

Elenid Jones

Our Gifts for Jesus

Some of the children of Manod junior school, Blaenau Ffestiniog, were asked what gift they would give to Jesus if he was born today:

Daniel:
If Jesus was born today I would give him a computer so that he could e-mail messages to everyone.

Llinos Griffiths:
If Jesus was born today I would give him some comfortable shoes as a gift.

Ashley:
If Jesus was born today I would give him a Bible as a present so that he could look back at his life two thousand years ago.

Clare:
If Jesus was born today I would give him a gold pot, full of money because everything is so expensive today.

Kiki:
If Jesus was born today I would give him a horse as a gift. As a little boy he could play with it, and when he grows up he could use it to travel around Wales.

Llinos Orton:
If Jesus was born today I would give him a gold necklace with his name engraved on it.

Gweno:
If Jesus was born today I would give him a Bible so that he could read all about himself when he was in the world before.

Ben:
If Jesus was born today I would give him a computer as a present to help him write and talk to people everywhere.

Sioned Humphreys:
If Jesus was born today I would give him a bike and a helmet as a gift. It took hours to travel from place to place on the back of that old donkey. A bike would get him around much faster. On the front of the bike I would put a basket so that he could carry things safely in it.

Thea:
If Jesus was born today I would give him an expensive toy angel as it was an angel that told the world about his birth.

Emma:
If Jesus was born today I would give him some brand new clothes as a present. He hadn't any clothes to keep him cosy and warm when he came to the world before.

Here are some of the hopes of the children of Manod again for the new millennium

Vicky:
Everyone to stop fighting, to keep God's laws and to share things more fairly.

Caitlin:
No wasting the environment, no more tree felling and no endangering the world's wildlife.

Michael:
No war nor disasters like tornadoes or earthquakes to kill innocent people.

Bryn:
I would like to see all the people of the world being friends.

Ellen Mair:
People to share their wealth with the poor people of the world.

Sarah:
I would like to see the world a more happy and contented place.

Llyr:
No war, tornadoes, earthquakes or volcanoes to kill people.

Ffion Griffith:
Everyone praying before going to bed to thank God for all the things they have received.

Caryl:
I would like to see a world without money so people would be more prepared to share with others.

Iwan Michelmore:
Everyone in the world with a comfortable home and plenty of food.

Janine:
No more wars, everyone to be happy and the world's animals to be able to live naturally.

Ffion Haf:
Everyone sharing; being friends and ending wars; plenty of food for everyone; and everyone respecting the world.

HERE I AM IN 2000

Name: ....

Address: ....

....

....

Other members of my family: ....

....

....

Here I am   Here are my Family

Here's what happened on January 1st, 2000:

....

....

....

....

Here are a few of the things in the news:

....

....

....

....

....

....

....

....

....

My friends: ....

....

....

My school: ....

My teachers: ....

Other things I belong to: ....

....

I live in: ....

Population of the area: ....

Here is a picture of my house:

SOME OF MY FAVOURITE THINGS IN 2000

Favourite food: ....

....

Favourite music : ....

Favourite saying : ....

Favourite place : ....

Favourite games : ....

....

Favourite toy : ....

Favourite Tv programme(s) : ....

....

Favourite game : ....

PHOTOS OF 2000

New car

Fashionable clothes in 2000

My Favourite food

My Favourite computer game

WHAT HAPPENED DURING 2000

January:

February:

March:

April:

May:

June:

July:

August:

September:

October:

November:

December:

IN THE YEAR 2000

COST OF A PACKET OF CRISPS:

COST OF A BURGER AND CHIPS:

COST OF A PINT OF MILK:

COST OF A CAN OF COKE

COST OF A NEWSPAPER:

COST OF A COMIC:

SOCCER CHAMPIONS:

WIMBLEDON CHAMPIONS:

SNOOKER WORLD CHAMPION:

SOME POP GROUPS IN THE CHARTS: